Legends

of

EXMOOR

Jack Hurley

The Exmoor Press

First printed 1973. Reprinted 1976, 1980, 1988, 1993 and 1997

ISBN 0 900131 09 8

★

MICROSTUDIES

Each Microstudy has been written by an expert and is designed to appeal to all who are interested in Exmoor.

A list of all the titles is available from

The Exmoor Press   Dulverton   Somerset

Trade sales enquiries:
HALSGROVE
Halsgrove House
Lower Moor Way
Tiverton, EX16 6SS
Tel: 01884 243242
Fax: 01884 243325

★

Printed in Great Britain by Williton Printers, Somerset

Contents

Drawings

Front Cover
Mother Leakey (see also page 26)   George Cruikshank

Inside Front Cover
Four Flowers of Legend   Audrey Wilson
  a. Foxglove—grows the gloves worn by foxes to stalk their prey.
  b. Greater Celandine—is an eye medicine. Swallows pluck it for their young who are born blind.
  c. Lords and Ladies—symbolise procreation.
  d. Daffodil—is among the first to greet the return to earth of the goddess of spring.

Throughout the text   Audrey Wilson

The Author

The late Jack Hurley wrote *Murder and Mystery on Exmoor* and *Snow and Storm on Exmoor* in the Microstudy series. He was also the author of *Rattle his Bones* (an historical study of Exmoor workhouses) and of *Exmoor in Wartime.* Jack's life and work, first as a reporter and then as editor of the *West Somerset Free Press,* form the subject of a chapter in the Microstudy, *Exmoor Writers,* by Victor Bonham-Carter. ˙

Acknowledgements

My interest in legend and lore was stimulated many years ago by an esteemed and senior colleague in journalism, the late Herbert W. Kille, of Minehead, who made local history his hobby. To him I owe my introduction to several homes of legend mentioned in this book, notably Combe Sydenham, Bardon and Sandhill. Especially do I remember the fascination with which I listened to his pixie yarns, and discussed with him the results of his researches into the stories of Tom Faggus. In connection with the illustrations in this book I wish to thank the owners of properties and incumbents of churches. Mr. E. G. Campbell-Vouillaire has been a most valuable informant on Combe Sydenham, which property he formerly owned.

J.H.

The Ponds at Combe Sydenham c. 1900

(H. H. Hole)

4

Introduction

Legends are like stalks that have grown out of a grain of truth and have remained waving like a magic wand. It is difficult to grasp them cleanly without something else coming away in one's hand . . . a bit of ghost, a little lore, or the root of a tradition. The extraneous cannot be discarded; indeed, it contributes to the legend's weight. For this reason I have tried to examine the backgrounds against which the legends in this book are set. In nearly every story a certain amount of fact is a foundation. In the exceptions, such as the pixie and the woman-into-hare tales, one must admire the old storytellers for such a display of conviction that one feels like apologising for a disbelieving mind!

The purest legend inventions, perhaps, are the very extremes . . . the Devil and his astonishing physical labours on the one hand; the early Christian saints and their adventures on the other. The rubber of 20th century scepticism never succeeds entirely in erasing a legend. Perversely, and rather delightfully, traditional belief has usually defeated reasoned argument. An ecclesiastical commission of inquiry may pronounce that a certain widow never re-appeared after her death, yet it fails to kill the belief at the time, and cannot expunge the legend. No treasure is buried under Exmoor's famous Caractacus stone, but that does not stop a secretive visit to the place by night, and an apparent attempt to start a dig. In the 20th century, too! An Elizabethan cannonball flies thousands of miles to land at the portals of an old mansion. Nonsense? Yet on a 20th century occasion an almost fearful mark of respect is shown for the story!

Did the Exmoor farmer always thresh his own corn . . . or was he helped by the little pixie people? What broke an attic window of Bardon House? Stone-throwing by youngsters . . . or was it the tapping of a mysterious white dove enshrining the spirit of a be-headed queen?

The aim of this book, a collection of legend, lore, and inevitably a few ghostly attachments, is escapism for the reader into imagination's airy uplands. Exmoor has many waymarked walks, but beware capricious pixies who may still confound the signs and lead walkers from Dan to Beersheba instead of from Mounsey to Mousehanger!

The Doones of Exmoor have been deliberately excluded from this book. However, the case for one of the Lorna Doone characters, highwayman Tom Faggus, fact or fiction, is examined, for Tom is capable of leading an existence independent of Blackmore's story.

1 The White Dove of Bardon

Is there a prettier legend than one showing a pure white dove as the spirit of a dead Queen?

A dove that flies where trees crowd into a shade around an ancient manor house. Flies purposefully to an attic window, taps with its beak and beats its wings.

Taps again, through days and weeks, insistent upon a response. And harder. Until one day it breaks the window.

Is there something in this attic to which attention is being drawn?

* * * * *

Secluded Bardon House lies at the north-east corner of Exmoor National Park, in the parish of Old Cleeve. Probably it has been a homestead from very early times, for Bardon is a variation of Barton, deriving from the Anglo-Saxon 'beretun', corn farm. But it was during its long occupancy by successive generations of the Leigh family of lawyers, beginning some 400 years ago, that Bardon achieved notice on three counts, with a dramatic climax in 1836. These counts are legend, historical fact with which legend has been interwoven, and ghosts.

Master of Bardon in 1836 was Robert Leigh, one of the long lawyer line. One day the servants reported that an attic window was broken, and Leigh ordered its repair. But a few days later he was annoyed to be told that the window was again broken, and this time the servants had a strange story. They had seen a white dove fly repeatedly against the pane. Leigh was incredulous. He was disposed to blame stone-throwing by young gardeners, but the servants held to their story; the window breaker was a white dove.

At length, Leigh decided to take a look in the attic. He noticed an old box and had it opened. Inside were documents which had nothing to do with any legal affairs known to him. And they raised a mystery. Why were they in Bardon House at all?

The Babington Plot

Leigh had found State papers, and at the time of their writing they must have been of vital importance. State papers, found in an obscure country house 160 miles from London, through the window-breaking agency of a white dove? Legend and mystery were conjoined. Examination showed the papers to concern the relations between Queen Elizabeth I and Mary Queen of Scots, after the latter had become a virtual prisoner in England in 1568. They were also a commentary on the Babington Plot against the life of Elizabeth, and presented in a way that implicated Mary right up to her pretty neck, on which the executioner's axe fell in 1587. These writings spared nothing that would bring Mary's past to remembrance. They set forth her supposed misdeeds; every circumstance that could be contrived to her detriment had been entered. But they also contained Mary's denial of the allegations.

The historical value of such documents was plain, and in 1870 the British Museum acquired them from Bardon. Dr. Charles Cotton, who married into the Leigh family, edited them, and they were printed in the Camden Society publications, third series, No. 7, 1909.

The Pretty Fancy

The attachment of both legend and mystery to the facts make the Bardon story. First, the white dove. Did it really appear? According to more than one servant, it did. And it becomes one of the prettiest fancies in the realm of legend . . . the spirit of Mary Queen of Scots taking the form of a dove, white to denote innocence, and seeking to draw attention to the whereabouts of documents containing her denial of the treason with which she was charged. The legend binds those very documents that are historical fact and are now registered as 'The Bardon Papers'.

One may ask why the ill-starred Queen, in her dove-like form, waited centuries to have the papers discovered. But if all things could be explained, how naked would Lady Legend become! It has been assumed that the papers had lain at Bardon a great many years, and there is no answer to the question of queenly patience. But after the discovery the dove appeared no more to beat its wings against the window pane.

The Throckmortons

One mystery propounds another. Why were such papers in a West Country house that had no connection with national events of the time? One suggestion borders on the just possible. The papers were in a container known as the 'Throckmorton Box'. One of the Bardon Leighs had been lawyer to Sir Robert Throckmorton, who owned property in the immediate locality and also on the southern edge of Exmoor, at Molland—where the family is still known. In the intrigues surrounding Queen Elizabeth's throne, Throckmorton—like Babington—was a familiar and sinister name.

There was Francis Throckmorton, a zealous Catholic, who engaged in plots abroad against the English government, and was arrested in England while acting as confidential agent of a conspiracy for the invasion of this country by a French army. The purpose was to release Mary Queen of Scots and set her on the throne in place of Elizabeth, who was to be assassinated. Francis Throckmorton, or what was left of him after the hideous pattern of torture in the Tower of London, was executed at Tyburn. His brother, Thomas, settled in Paris as an agent of Mary. Another of the family, Sir Nicholas, although a Protestant, is said to have believed in the justice of Mary's claim to the English throne, and to have succumbed to her personal charm.

Perhaps these papers came into the possession of the Throckmorton family generations after the recorded events, and were sent to repose with the family's lawyer at Bardon, there forgotten until a white dove drew attention to them in 1836.

Historical Underlining

The papers throw much light on the trial of Mary. They are the historical underlining of the white dove legend. Small wonder that the spirit of the Queen was so insistent upon their discovery.

In 1584, Queen Elizabeth's ministers, particularly Burleigh and Walsingham, intensified their vigilance in detecting conspiracies. They composed counterfeit letters in Mary Queen of Scots' name and had them delivered into the homes of Roman Catholics, for Walsingham ran a very efficient establishment of spies and informers.

When Mary was finally tried for complicity in the Babington Plot against Elizabeth, a letter purporting to have been sent by Mary to Babington played a vital part in bringing her to the headsman's block. But the letter had been concocted in Walsingham's office, and Mary's signature had been forged. Her friends maintained, even at their peril, that the letter was a fabrication.

The Ghosts

As if the white dove legend, coupled with historical fact, were not enough for one house, Bardon has been noted for its ghosts. According to one tradition, one of the Leighs has been a wanderer in the grounds, carrying a head (not his own) under his arm. The Bardon coach and horses arrive with a crunch of wheels and hooves on the gravel drive. Sound without vision, this, but reported in recent years when Mr. and Mrs. Edward Collier were in residence. And in the house has been heard plaintive music, as might be drawn from a spinet or harpsichord. Doubtless, the player is the white-haired lady of sorrowful countenance, who is wont to glide through the rooms in a dress of rustling silk.

Among the outdoor phantoms is the inevitable black dog, a manifestation that legend makes common to several places on Exmoor. It is a curious facet of Bardon history that the house, so long the abode of lawyers, continued as such after the Leighs had gone. The last Leigh instructed Thomas Ponsford in law there, and he became principal of a firm of solicitors which is in practice at Williton today as Risdon and Company. Thomas Joyce, who lived at Bardon, and was a former partner in the solicitors' firm, claimed to have seen the black dog on the lawn, and he recounted the incident to Clement Kille, a journalist who wrote for the *West Somerset Free Press.* Another sighting was claimed by a member of the Leigh family, Miss Katherine St. B. Leigh; she, in 1922, told Clement Kille's son, Herbert.

Exorcism

That the Bardon spirits had been exorcised early in the 19th century by seven parsons with bell, book and candle, was another story told to Clement Kille by an old local inhabitant. The parsons caused the spirits to assume the form of a black dog. A servant seized the animal, put a halter about its neck, and threw it into the nearest pond. The parsons had charged the servant not to look behind him after disposing of the dog, but, like Lot's wife, he could not resist a peep. Lo! The pond was all aflame. Obviously, the exorcism was none too successful, for the black dog was able to appear to Thomas Joyce many years later!

Bardon has never lost its reputation for ghosts. In recent years the TV cameras have tried to capture them, but they have been exceeding shy.

Pass the drive to the house, and you may see a white shape flit soundlessly from a tree. Sorry! Not a white dove making for an attic window. Just an owl after a mouse.

9

2 Buy a House . . . Buy its Legend

Lot 67 in a catalogue of sale . . . 'Quantity of antlers and a cannon-ball'.

Forget the antlers that had been worn by Exmoor red deer and were now oddly bracketed with a cannonball. Here was legend at its most romantic, reduced to three words in a sale catalogue . . . 'and a cannonball'.

It was November 1950. Squire Marwood Notley was ending his family's 150 years ownership of Combe Sydenham, the hall that, before the Notleys, had been one of the homes of the ubiquitous Sydenham family for nearly four centuries. And with the removal of the last Notley squire from ancestral home to modern bungalow close by, it looked as though the visible link with a famous legend might be leaving also.

The link was that cannonball, Lot 67 in the auction of the Combe Sydenham furniture and effects. Local people were surprised. Selling Sir Francis Drake's cannonball? The one he fired from Plymouth to land at Combe as a warning to Elizabeth Sydenham not to marry another suitor? Or the 'thing' that came from the skies?

No good would come of selling this relic, said the old folk around Combe. And of what use would the cannonball be to a purchaser who took it away? Was it realised that, no matter where it was taken, it would roll back to Combe Sydenham?

Here we sense relish and respect for legend, and they were about to be recognised. On the day of the Combe sale it was announced that the 'Drake cannonball' had been withdrawn from the catalogue and would 'go with the house'. It had gone with the house for nearly four centuries . . . an oddity among the Chippendale and the tapestries, the paintings and the Queen Anne and Georgian silver.

The cannonball had been entered in the sale catalogue by mistake, and Mr. Marwood Notley rectified it as soon as his attention was drawn to it. The ball had found mention in Combe Sydenham property deeds from Sydenham family times.

Elizabethans

Among the Sydenhams the house had known were Sir George and his daughter and heiress, Elizabeth, to whom Sir Francis Drake paid court. He married her (she was his second wife) in 1585, in nearby Monksilver church. Combe Sydenham Hall, much altered and reduced since its stately Elizabethan days, is worth seeing through the eyes of Richard Jefferies, that graceful writer who succumbed to the fascination of Exmoor. He wrote of a manor house without naming it, but he gave a clue when he mentioned that under the table on the stone floor of the hall was 'Sir Francis

10

Drake's cannonball'. How charged with atmosphere is Jefferies' description of Combe in his two-part book *Round About A Great Estate* and *Red Deer* (published 1884).

There is an old hall with a knight's helmet carved above the porch. The black oak door stands ajar, so massive and heavy with iron rivets that no gust of air can stir it. A wind comes from the woods, and entering a vaulted passage strays aside freely into the dwelling rooms. For the door in the passage is also ajar, being in like manner of thick oak, iron studded and unmoved.

Within, the high windows, set deep in the wall, do but just overcome with all their light the heavy weight of the black oak furniture. Dark oak shutters, dark oak window seats, dark oak beams overhead, a black table in the midst of the great room, oak cabinets and lesser tables, all engrained with age . . . The very polish of the oak is lustreless, it is smooth, but does not reflect. Old shadowy days of rapier and ruff, armour and petronnel, days when the Spanish Main was on all men's lips; of Sir Francis Drake, whose cannon still sound in the hottest hours of summer . . . there is a dream in every chair; romance grown richer with age like the colour of the oak; forth from the iron studded door go the cavalier and his lady a-hawking.

How Did It Come?

It is upon romance that the cannonball legend relies for its perennial appeal . . . that the marriage between Elizabeth Sydenham and Sir Francis Drake was a real love match. That alone has inspired the romantic story of a dramatic intervention that preserved a loving couple for each other.

The legend poses puzzle. How did this 'cannonball' object come to Combe? Is it a cannonball, or is it a meteorite, of cannonball size, which crashed to earth during a thunderstorm? And did it come as a divine sign in answer to a lady's prayer?

Cannonball it is in written tradition, but at one hundredweight the object is far heavier than a cannonball of the same size would be.

Elizabeth Sydenham was Drake's second wife, and she was about 18 years old when the marriage took place. Versions of the cannonball legend are as varied as they are numerous, and the one given in this chapter was the favourite with the Notley family. Indeed, it was written out in the 19th century by a Mrs. Notley, who was critical of a version that had appeared in a London magazine.

As told by Mrs. Notley, the story begins with Sir George and Lady Sydenham being strongly against the romance that was developing between their daughter and Francis Drake; they would have preferred as a husband for their daughter a wealthy suitor who lived at Orchard Wyndham, Williton. However, Elizabeth defied opposition, and ran away and married Drake. The deed being done, there was little point in the Sydenhams remaining unforgiving, and Elizabeth came home to Combe Sydenham to remain under her parents' care while the adventurous Drake was away on one of his long sea voyages.

Long Silence

Nothing was heard of Drake for several years, and Elizabeth may have begun to reflect that her parents' judgment had been better than hers when they had pressed her not to marry the reckless

11

seaman. There were whispers from the outside world that Drake and his crew had perished at sea, and Elizabeth was now having to resist the advice tendered to her to consider herself a widow. It was a belief of the times that if a husband and wife heard nothing of each other for seven years they were free to marry again, even if there was no certainty that death had parted them.

The original suitor for Elizabeth's hand, the young man from Orchard Wyndham, came upon the scene again (to the delight of Sir George and Lady Sydenham), and eventually Elizabeth yielded to the now familiar pressures . . . she agreed that when seven years were up she would marry the Orchard Wyndham suitor.

Yet her heart had been always with Drake, and something told her that he lived. No word came, the seven years ran out, and the young woman steeled herself to keep her promise and to marry the man her parents had always wanted for her. Preparations for the wedding were made. Still an inner voice told Elizabeth that Drake was alive. On the wedding morning she prayed that if Drake was alive God would send her some token of it and so spare her the sin and misery of a false and perjured marriage. Calmed by her prayer, strangely assured in her heart that it had been heard and would be answered, Elizabeth allowed her maids to robe her in her bridal dress and went downstairs to meet the guests and the bridegroom.

Between Them

The young man took her hand to lead her from the hall, and at that moment a cannonball rolled between them. No-one had seen the manner of its coming. The clasped hands dropped, and Elizabeth cried out that the ball was the token for which she had prayed; Drake was alive. Rushing upstairs, she locked herself in her room and refused to leave it.

· That same day Drake's ships put into Plymouth Sound. All the countryside said he had fired the cannonball from Plymouth so that his wife would know he was alive and coming to her with all speed. But, says the family version of the story, the strange ball was never fired from any cannon. It came from the sky in answer to Elizabeth's prayer.

The ball, finding a settled place in the hall at Combe Sydenham, inevitably trimmed itself with a tradition . . . that if moved it would always return to the same spot under the hall table. Several stories have made the point, some told by members of the Notley family and their retainers.

A housekeeper, showing the cannonball to a visitor, rolled it out from beneath the hall table, telling her visitor to observe that it made 'a noise like thunder', and that when rolled back again it 'knew its place' and settled on the identical spot from which it was started.

Down The Hill . . . Naturally!

The ball weighs about an hundredweight. Another amusing 'it always rolls home' story comes from the time when James Thomas

12

Benedictus Notley, who died in 1851, was squire at Combe Sydenham. He is said to have been singularly impressed by a demonstration put on by a few of his workmen. They put the cannonball in a sack, lugged it up a steep field, then turned it loose. It ran back to the house. It was hardly likely to run uphill, was it? Yet the demonstration seemed to impress the watching squire, or was it the shout of his workmen, 'There you are, squire, cannonball's going home, like 'tis said!' Anyway, the squire ordered cider all round.

This little tale may be as legendary as the main one!

In A Play

The legend makes excellent theatre. Playwright Phoebe Rees, whose home was at Nettlecombe Rectory, midway between the two houses of Combe Sydenham and Bardon, incorporated the legends of both in plays. Her series of one-act dramas for women includes *Marriages Are Made In Heaven*, which is based on the Combe Sydenham story. Laurence Housman, playwright of *Victoria Regina* fame, wrote an amusing foreword.

'I am anxious that the cannonball should have been truly of Drake's sending', Housman said. 'Either it arrived in a thunderstorm, sent down from Heaven above, or it came up through the torn bowels of Mother Earth from Drake himself. To materialistic minds, both explanations seem equally impossible; but, as the cannonball cannot be explained away, how did it come? And as this play calls upon us to believe two impossibilities, then I very much prefer to believe that it was not Heaven, but Drake, that sent it!'

Appropriately, *Marriages Are Made In Heaven* was given its first performance in 'Drake Town' . . . by the Plymouth Towns-women's Guild.

Original House

Combe Sydenham, one of the oldest houses in the National Park, was built by Sir John Sydenham in c. 1360. There was an Elizabethan re-building by Sir George Sydenham, Elizabeth's father. Originally, the house had two or three towers; now there is one. The entrance, dated 1580, and a gracefully arched gateway, are probably the only unaltered remains of Sir George Sydenham's house.

After Mr. Marwood Notley, Combe Sydenham passed into the ownership of Mr. E. G. Campbell-Vouillaire, in whose time considerable restoration was carried out. Upon leaving Combe, Mr. Campbell-Vouillaire had the famous cannonball placed in the county museum at Taunton. Thus, for the first time since its mysterious arrival, the ball left the hall. Of course, its safe repose in the museum knocks for six the 'rolling back' stories, but these were always for entertainment rather than belief! One of them was that the ball, if carried away and thrown into the deepest of the Combe Sydenham ponds, would be found again in the hall at break of day.

But although the ball has been moved, the romantic heart of the legend remains undisturbed . . . the sign from heaven in answer to Elizabeth Sydenham's prayer.

13

3 Lived Once . . . Buried Twice

Night . . . and across the fields a tiny, moving glimmer from a lantern. Who walks at this hour? The figure is a woman, and she wears the habiliments of the grave.

But this is no horror story, the figure no phantom. Here is the living flesh and blood of Florence Wyndham, the lady of Kentsford Manor. Here is legend at its most joyous. Someone is coming back from the grave.

Florence Wyndham . . . lived once, buried twice. First, in a death-like trance, to be awakened by a sexton who entered the tomb vault with the object of stealing the rings from her fingers.

Diffidently would a writer label this story as pure legend, for it is woven into the history of an ancient and prominent English family, members of whom have, both orally and in writing, placed credence upon it. There are descendants who hold that they would not be here but for Florence Wyndham's return from the tomb, and the fact that subsequently she bore a son to her husband John.

The Risk

The story has been told in every generation around the north-east border of Exmoor for the last 400 years. Basically, it is by no means incredible. Centuries ago it was a risk that sick people, passing into an unconscious or trance-like state, might be presumed dead. This is the Florence Wyndham story.

If it is accepted that here was just one person lucky to escape death in a premature tomb because a thieving sexton intervened, then the story becomes merely a shivery piece of the macabre, something that caused old ladies to twitch their shawls more closely around their shoulders as they told it. But to view it like that is to rob it of legendary or romantic touch.

Location

Kentsford can be reached on a walk northwards along the track of the old West Somerset Mineral Railway. A mile from Watchet is Kentsford level crossing, a spot to which the fine old manor dwelling (now a farmhouse) on the other side of the hedge, gives its name.

It is Wyndham family history that helps to give the Kentsford story of the lady Florence its legendary lift, for the event of 400 years ago may have ensured the continuance of the name.

In the 16th century, Florence Wadham, sister of Nicholas Wadham, the man who founded Wadham College, Oxford, married John Wyndham, of Orchard Wyndham, Williton, and they took over Kentsford manor house, two miles away. In 1559 Florence was taken seriously ill, lapsed into a coma which in those days was called a trance, and was taken for dead. She was buried in the family vault in St. Decuman's church, Watchet, on the hill above Kentsford.

At Dead Of Night

The sexton, knowing that valuable rings had been left on the lady's fingers, resolved to acquire them, and at dead of night he put his covetous intent into action. Carrying a lantern, he entered the vault.

The story attracts a number of variations. According to the most popular account the sexton, unable to pull the rings from the stiff fingers, began to use a knife. To his horror, he saw the blood flow and the body stir. He fled the church, dropping his lantern. Some versions make this the moment for retribution. They give us a sexton so overcome by terror that he turns into a gibbering madman; rushing down the hill into Watchet, he throws himself into the sea.

There is no point in following Nemesis down there! We can stay at the church to see Florence Wyndham, now completely out of her trance . . . and out of her coffin. She picks up the sexton's lantern and walks down over the fields to Kentsford, to beat upon the door for admittance. Some difficulty over this, naturally. Who would dream of letting in a ghost? But Florence convinces her husband she is real, and the door closes upon a couple experiencing the joyful miracle of reunion.

15

Family Chronicles

In the 1930s two volumes on Wyndham family history, by the Hon. H. A. Wyndham, were published. The author refers to the Kentsford story thus: 'A peculiar and disturbing contingency was that but for the covetousness of the sexton moving him to interfere with the supposed corpse, the family of Wyndham might have become extinct in the male line, for every living member of it is descended from the one child, John, born after her (Florence's) resurrection.'

In those chronicles the sexton is named as Attewell. About twelve years ago the present writer interviewed Walter John Prole, then aged 90, retired sexton at St. Decuman's, a post with which his family had been connected for generations, and he mentioned that his paternal grandmother was an Attewell. It is a name that has persisted in Watchet for centuries, and is found there today.

The first Wyndhams came to prominence and power in Norfolk in the mid-15th century, but when in 1502 Sir John Wyndham was executed for high treason, it seemed that they were back where they started, with little hope of recouping their lands, position or influence. For many families it would have been the end, but the Wyndhams were so resilient that inside a generation they had re-covered lost ground and re-entered the councils and courts of power. They consolidated and spread, made the marriages and connections that mattered . . . with great families like Howard, Scrope, Dudley, Seymour and Percy . . . and for centuries there was always a Wyndham in the English tapestry of war and peace, politics and power. The family spread into many branches, and by the 18th century there were seven to the candelabra which had had a Norfolk base. The Hon. H. A. Wyndham calls it 'a rise based on the complex pyramid of marriage sales, manorial rights, messuages and moieties'.

Locally the family is represented today by Dr. K. S. H. Wyndham, she is the daughter of the late Mr. George Wyndham, of Orchard Wyndham, Williton.

It might be thought that Florence Wyndham must have been cutting a classic figure as a ghost down through the centuries. Not so. She does not walk the fields, or haunt the place of her premature entombment. She walked but once . . . in 1559, as living flesh, her blood set re-coursing by a sexton who unwittingly ensured a family's future.

Bardon Manor

Combe Sydenham House

(H. H. Hole)

Brass of John and Florence Wyndham in St. Decuman's, Watchet
(Colin Thornton)

Bench End, alleged to represent Florence Wyndham, at St. George's,
Sampford Brett

(Colin Thornton)

St. Dubricius, Porlock

(Iris Hardwick)

4 The Indestructible Mother Shipton

When ships use the truncated spire of the church of St. Dubricius at Porlock as a mooring post, the fairest vale below Exmoor will have vanished beneath the Channel waters. Perish the thought! The inundation of Porlock and a resultant maritime role for the top of the church spire was one of the alleged prophecies of the famous Mother Shipton who, though born near Knaresborough, in Yorkshire, has obtained a strange hold on the minds of people living on the eastern borders of Exmoor. They have even allocated her a tomb in a wood near Williton and she seems to be honoured in the fashion of Homer, whom half-a-dozen places in Greece claimed for native!

Mother Shipton, whose prophecies, in number and range, out-ran those of Holy Writ, is lodged as securely in local legend as a limpet upon a rock.

As a prophetess, Mother Shipton became a best-seller. The 17th century pamphleteers who handled her rhymed utterances could have vouched for that. And if there was anything upon which she did not prophetically pronounce, her enterprising publishers could always make good the deficiency. They needed only a knack for composing prophetic jingles in two or four-line measure.

To this day, people hold perversely that Mother Shipton belonged to the Exmoor borders. She was born Ursula Sontheil, a mis-shapen child with large, goggling eyes, a long, crooked nose, and crooked legs. Her birthplace is said to have been a cave which is now one of the show places of Knaresborough. Her birth year was 1472, and at the age of 24 she married a Toby Shipton. She established a reputation for insight into the future, and people for miles around came to consult her. She died about 1561.

The writer went, when a boy, in quest of Mother Shipton's 'tomb', and found it, a mile from where this account is being written. He would have spared himself the trouble, had he known at the time that the 'tomb' had been exposed as a spurious stone as long ago as 1879.

But no-one shall expose Mother Shipton . . . or dispose of her!

Dire Forecasts

Two prophecies, each concerning the Exmoor coastline, de-termined that Mother Shipton should win her footing here in legend. One was the dire forecast, already mentioned, of Porlock going under the waters. The other has jingled in the minds of many generations of Williton and Watchet folk:

21

Watchet and Doniford both shall drown,
And Williton become the seaport town.

Coast erosion, anyway, is always a safe bet for prognostication. In this instance it has served to increase Mother Shipton's authoritative standing, for in the late 19th century and the early 20th the Watchet-Doniford coastline suffered a quite alarming recession. It brought the sea to within a few yards of the railway line, and at Doniford wiped away the slipway and cliffside donkey houses associated with the ancient lime-burning industry. It was common to hear old people say: 'Ah! Remember Mother Shipton? Her words are coming true'.

But in the Porlock Vale there were, thankfully, no signs of farmers preparing to turn sailors. World championship barley continued to be raised there.

The Loyalists

Mother Shipton had become peculiarly West Somerset. And there she stays. *Encyclopaedia Britannica* is cautious about her: 'No trustworthy evidence . . . her whole history rests on the flimsiest authority'.

That will not do for the Mother Shipton loyalists. Early in the 17th century, some 80 years after her death, she received nationwide publicity through the issue of a pamphlet containing her alleged prophecies. It was an extraordinary catalogue of jingles on scores of diversified subjects, and covering many places throughout the land. Whether they are by Mother Shipton or the crafty hand of the pamphleteers or distributors, the prophecies make entertaining reading, and they duly appeared in a second and enlarged edition. This time there was one foretelling the end of the world in 1881. This event was given a West Country locale. Someone deduced that the first signs of crack-up would appear at Ham Hill, in Somerset, on Good Friday.

Contemporary newspaper accounts show that the prediction caused a sensation in Somerset. Many people evinced a fearful belief. Some inhabitants around Ham Hill took themselves off to distant parts; others removed their breakable possessions and ceased to cultivate their gardens. Good Friday passed at Ham Hill . . . and everywhere else . . . without a sign of cataclysm. Mother Shipton caught out this time? No, said her unswerving loyalists. The pamphleteers must have got the date wrong!

Slab In A Wood

At some stage, probably in the 18th century, Williton laid claim to Mother Shipton as its native, and declared that her tomb was to be seen in a nearby wood.

This makes a mystery on its own. It is true that in Blackdown

22

Wood, between Williton and Nettlecombe, there had long been a stone slab bearing an inscription in Latin. Investigations in 1879 showed that the stone is a fake; a copy, made probably in the 18th century, of a sepulchral Roman slab on an estate in Cumberland, belonging at one time to the Wyndham family. The inscription on the spurious stone was copied from a sketch of the real article, and this was done by the author of a book published in 1726. The inscription on the Cumberland slab is: *Dis manibus Julia Martima vixit annos doudecim menses tres dies viginti duos.* The English translation reads: *To the gods of the shades; Julia Martima lived twelve years, three months, and 22 days.* That is to say, the original stone commemorates a young Roman girl who went to the shades some 15 centuries ago. The Blackdown Wood stone shows a wreath; there is none on the original. So it would seem that the sculptor of the copy, finding he had a blank space, looked through his pattern book and selected a wreath to fill it. Thus we have the imitation memorial stone to a young Roman girl decorated with a triumphal wreath that would have been assigned only to a Roman general!

The mystery remains. Why was a copy of a Cumberland slab placed in a West Somerset wood? No explanation has ever been forthcoming.

Mother Shipton continued to bestride the local world of legend like a female Colossus. Even modern guide books have picked her up and blandly buried here 'near the high road at Williton, close to the Orchard Wyndham mansion'. Like Arthur, she cannot be extinguished.

5 The Whistler of the Wind

On November 5, 1634, Susan Leakey, a widow, was buried in Minehead churchyard.

None too successfully, it would seem, for she was soon around the old seaport town again . . . 'in her full proportion and usual apparel'. The latter consisted of 'a black gown, a white stomacher of shagge, and a kercher on her head'.

It was very disconcerting. People will sometimes tolerate a mild-mannered apparition as an old friend, but in Mother Leakey Minehead had acquired a termagent spirit bent on mischief—ranging from an unladylike kicking of a gentleman's backside to whistling up Channel storms that wrecked ships.

Distressing as well as disconcerting, because Mother Leakey in her materialisations was the exact antithesis of what she had been in life . . . a mild, good-natured woman, a regular churchgoer.

Ominous Forecast

Indeed, so well liked was Mother Leakey, so genial in company, that her friends thought it a thousand pities that the time should ever come for her to depart this life. They told her so, and were mightily disturbed when she replied: 'Forasmuch as you now seem to like me, I am afraid you will but little care to see or speak with me after my death, though I believe you may have that satisfaction'.

In the legends of her troublesome appearances, her words came only too true. She was sufficiently notorious for Sir Walter Scott to mention her in his notes on 'Rokeby'; he described her as 'the most formidable whistler he ever remembered to have met with'. This was a reference to Mother Leakey's appearances on the quay at Minehead for the purpose of whistling up storms to endanger the shipping. That her son Alexander, a well-to-do mariner, whose ships traded between Minehead and Ireland, might be one of the sufferers, was apparently of no account; in fact, he was reduced to ruin. It is recorded that 'his fair estate was all buried in the sea, and he that was once worth thousands was reduced to a very low and poor condition'.

Commission Of Inquiry

Mother Leakey was getting out of hand. Three years after her death, the stories of her ghostly appearings were referred to the Bishop of Bath and Wells, who decided they must be investigated. He called in the Rev. Paul Godwin, Rector of Kingweston, and Sir Robert Phelipps, of Montacute, and the trio sat as a commission of inquiry.

They examined Elizabeth Leakey, wife of Alexander Leakey. Elizabeth said that her mother-in-law, on her deathbed, had told her she would reappear after death, not as a devil, but in the devil's likeness.

Elizabeth deposed that Mrs. Leakey had appeared several times to her . . . 'in full proportion and in her usual apparel'. On the last occasion Elizabeth had been bold to ask: 'Good mother, tell me whether you be in heaven or hell?' Mrs. Leakey had merely groaned in reply.

The second witness was the Minehead curate, Mr. Heathfield, who said that Mrs. Leakey had appeared to him one night as he was leaving Alexander Leakey's house. He admitted that he had previously been to a great christening feast!

No Credence

The commission disbelieved the curate, whom they described as a 'phantasticall' man. Neither were they disposed to accept Elizabeth Leakey's evidence.

Elizabeth Langston, another witness, deposed to Widow Leakey appearing 'as a little child, shining very bright and glorious'. Other people who would have been called to testify were not available; they seemed to have found it expedient to be elsewhere.

In this regard, the commission reported that an Italian mountebank, one Lencattelly, and a sailor, Garland, had claimed to have seen Mother Leakey. Warrants had been issued for both to attend the inquiry, but Lencattelly had gone from the town . . . 'we know not wither' . . . and Garland had gone to sea in one of Alexander Leakey's ships. Alexander himself was twice sent for, but he failed to appear, and the commission's comment was: 'The first time he was downe of the gowt and could not come, and the second time he absented himself from home for fear of executions which are out against him'.

The commission held no good opinion of any witness. Elizabeth Langston they described as 'a very silly and poor woman, very often distempered with drink, and doth not know that she sayeth'. They viewed Garland, the sailor, as an idle fellow, and considered that as he was employed by Alexander Leakey no credit could be given to his reports. Evidence had also been given by Elenor Fluellin, a servant to the Leakeys, but the commission set her down as 'a wanderer and a fit instrument to report anything that is put to her'.

Caught At The Stoop

The commission had not heard all the stories. One concerned a Minehead doctor who was walking in the fields when Mother Leakey appeared to him. He spoke to her civilly, and courteously handed her over a stile! She was in front of him at the next stile, planted herself upon it, and obstructed his passage. He got by with some difficulty, but while he was at the stoop Mother Leakey's toe caught him in the inviting place. This must have caused a severe loss of professional dignity.

The Bishop of Bath and Wells had heard first of Mother Leakey through that famous Royalist Rector of Luccombe, Dr. Henry Byam, into whose ears the people of the district had been pouring their tales.

Finally, the Bishop and his coadjutors delivered a judgment in the following terms: 'We are of opinion, and do believe, that there was never any such apparition at all, but that it was an imposture, devised and framed for some ends, but what they are we know not'. What were the Leakeys, and Curate Heathfield, who was so often in and out of their home, up to? Records of the case do not suggest a motive.

Archbishop Laud endorsed the judgment document on February 4, 1637, and it is among the State papers in the Public Record Office.

Legend With Wings

But the findings of a bishop's commission were powerless to kill the Leakey legend. It became one with wings that took the old bird up to the mainmasts of ships, where she perched to whistle up the winds and provoke great storms that destroyed vessels and cargoes. A gruesome story has it that she strangled her grandson John in his cradle, and that marks like the Devil's fingerprints were seen on the boy's neck. But records show that John died of consumption at the age of 14 . . . rather old for a cradle.

The Leakey legend lingered through the centuries, coming gradually to feature the old woman solely as a mariner's menace, and thus making her more distinctive, if less ubiquitous. The stories of her more domestic appearings and mischiefs dropped behind as time went by, leaving her pre-eminently a seaport's witch.

It was common, even in the early years of the present century, to hear the people of Minehead's quay town ascribe dirty weather to Mother Leakey's workings.

She, too, is as near-imperishable as legend can make anyone.

Cruikshank Drawing

The amusing drawing on the cover of this book, so perfectly capturing the incident of Mother Leakey and the doctor, is by George Cruikshank (1792—1878), the great caricaturist and illustrator of Dickens. His output was prolific and varied, and his book illustrations are justly famed.

6 The Ladies ran like Hares

Legend claims that hare hunters on the Brendon Hills had good sport with Fanny Pope, who kept an inn at Heathpoult Cross in the 19th century. Fanny would frequently turn herself into a hare, give the harriers their fun, then resume her human form and her occupation of selling beer. Customers would notice that she seemed somewhat breathless . . . as if she had been running!

Belief in witches entails acceptance of their familiar stock-in-trade of spells and stewpots, potions and prayers. Above all, of their strange powers, which could include self-transformation. Witch into hare was a particularly popular party turn.

Fanny's is a singular case because, though she acquired a witch's reputation, she did not spend her days as a black-hatted crone bent over a spell-pot. Aside from taking to the fields as a hare, she led a very practical existence as a dispenser of wallop to thirsty miners on the Brendons. Widow of the man who had kept the Poult Inn at the crossroads, Fanny carried on the trade. This lonely hill-country spot is now occupied by a bungalow.

Matter-of-Fact Belief

The once matter-of-fact belief that certain women were able to turn themselves into hares seems illustrated by an interview given to a journalist in 1922 by Tom Rawle, of Woodcombe, Minehead, and published in the *West Somerset Free Press*.

Tom was the son of John Rawle, huntsman for James Stoate, of Myne. In the early 19th century Stoate kept a pack of harehounds; this was the beginning of the hunt known today as the Minehead Harriers.

Tom Rawle was asked what was the longest hare hunt he could remember. He replied that it was from Oare, in around Porlock and back. They saw the hare jump up and go away in front of the hounds, and they never saw her afterwards.

Then came the significant remark: 'We thought that hare must be a witch. Those were the days when witches were about'!

That Oare-to-Porlock-and-back hare was certainly not Fanny Pope, who always operated within a convenient radius of the Poult Inn on the Brendons; it just goes to show that the Oare district had its own witch.

Old hill-country characters, who lived well into the 20th century, were telling the Fanny Pope legends to the end of their time . . . and convincing themselves, if not the pint buyers who were drawing them out.

Business Side

Cutcombe, the village below the Heathpoult hilltop, claimed Fanny Pope as a parishioner, and old characters took pride in passing on the tales about her. Fanny had a grandson who was in her confidence. He used to tell the master of hounds that he knew where they would find a hare that would give good sport. Invariably, it was Fanny who was put up; always she obliged the hunt with a splendid chase, whereupon the master would bestow a shilling upon the boy.

The system, profiting both boy and Fanny, was operated many times. The boy always ran with the harriers, and was alarmed one day when they got too close to their quarry. 'Urn, granny, urn, or they'll catch thee', he shouted. The hunt's suspicions were aroused, and they deepened when someone went into the Poult Inn and found Fanny panting as if from exhaustion. She had scratches upon her person, as if she had been through gorse or brambles.

The inevitable question arises. If hounds had caught their hare, would there have been a Fanny Pope to serve beer to the miners that night?

Readers should know better than to ask such a leading question in a court of legend!

Molly Of Oare

Another witch into hare legend has its location at Oare. It may account for Tom Rawle's story of the hare that ran from Oare into Porlock and back 'and they thought she must be a witch'.

In a lane below Oare Manor stood a holly tree and a gate which legend connected with a witch known as Molly. Few people liked to pass this place after dark for fear of seeing Molly, as a figure only six inches high, standing on the gate, or as a white hare in the lane.

28

Madam Carne

Probably the oldest local legend of this kind concerns Madam Joan Carne, of Sandhill, an ancient manor near Withycombe, on the northern side of Croydon Hill.

The lady is exceptionally good value. In addition to giving the run around as a hare, she is an upper class witch, a suspected disposer of one or more husbands, and she comes back to Sandhill after her own funeral to fry eggs and bacon. This is bonus legend indeed!

The present Sandhill dwelling, a farmhouse, is not earlier than 1558, but it derives from a manor dwelling which in 1100 belonged to the Honour of Dunster. Sandhill has evolved from the family name of de Sandell. The Sandells were tenants of the place up to the early 15th century, when they were replaced by the Newton family, of Swell, near Taunton; and it was a John Newton who in 1573 married the strange Joan of our story. She came from Dunster, and when John Newton died she married Charles Wyndham, one of the Orchard Wyndham, Williton, family. He did not last long, dying in 1585, whereupon twice-widowed Joan married Thomas Carne, of Evenny, Glamorgan, and gained the name in which she has become legendary.

Madam Joan Carne's three marriages are recorded on a brass in Withycombe church; however, there is no record to support the suspicions that she brought one or more of those husbands to a sticky end. But suspicions there were, and Joan Carne was evidently not a popular lady. She was believed to be a witch who used to transform herself into a white hare, and there is a story that a man caught and beat the hare one day. On the morrow, Madam Carne was seen with her head bandaged.

She died in 1612, and the most persistent story about her is that when the mourners returned to Sandhill after the funeral they found her spirit busy in the kitchen. Joan continued to haunt the house, and even in modern times there have been tales of curious manifestations in one of the rooms.

This should not be! For Joan's ghost was supposed to have been officially dismissed—'laid' in a Sandhill pond, whence her phantom figure issues once a year and takes a cockstride in the direction of Sandhill.

Squire's Story

The 'laying', in the early 19th century, had been a fiasco, according to a story which Squire Alexander Luttrell passed on to members of the West Somerset Archaeological Society when they held a meeting at Sandhill during the last war. Squire Luttrell had been told it by Thomas Ponsford, of Bardon, who is mentioned in the 'White Dove' chapter of this book.

Ponsford said Joan Carne's spirit was so troublesome that the local parsons decided they must exorcise it. News of the event brought out the whole countryside as spectators. The parsons came in caps and gowns, carrying bell, book and candle, and made for Sandhill pond. Behind them, the crowds of people were distinctly nervous. It needed only a man's shout, 'There her be', to start a panic. The people turned about and ran as if for their lives, and the parsons, throwing down their paraphernalia, ran too.

So Madam Carne reigned in possession. Sandhill, under successive farmers in the 19th and 20th centuries, became famous as a breeding ground for Devon cattle. Solid substance, those Red Rubies, but there is a story that one Sandhill farmer always kept a little room over the farmhouse porch furnished in readiness for Madam Carne's return from the pond!

Shivery

Was it with an instinct for atmosphere that local people identified as Joan Carne's pond the ugliest little pool of the several on the farm? Stagnant, sheeted in green slime, hooded by elders and willows . . . brooding a shiver. There, in 1883, journalist Clement Kille conversed with an old agricultural labourer whom he found to be sensitive to the surroundings and mindful of the tales that had been handed down.

Kille recorded the meeting in an article he wrote for the *West Somerset Free Press*. His dog had trotted to the pond's edge, when the old man broke off something he was saying to remark in his broad Somerset tongue: 'Excuse me, zur, ef I may-be zo bold, I'd call yer dawg back ef I waz you zur. Tes a wisht plaace, thic pond, a wisht plaace as ever anybody did mind on'.

Kille described his dog's behaviour thus: 'It stood intently gazing, with one of its forelegs uplifted and its ears pricked up; then, with a slight whine, it began to dabble at the edge of the water and then run round the margin as if it would have liked to make a closer acquaintance with some watery denizen.' Then, trembling with an excitement Kille had never noticed in him before, the dog again stood, as if fascinated, forefoot uplifted, body quivering.

Again the old labourer cried: 'Call un back, zur, call un back'. Then he told Kille the Madam Carne tale, emphasising that after her funeral she was back at Sandhill before the mourners, cooking for them, as described.

No Peace At All

'Vine works there waz vor months', said the old man. 'Nobody 'ad no peace at all wi' 'er a walkin' about th'ouse an' a laying 'er 'ands on everything. Things walked about in the queerest vashion you ever heered on, an' it zimmed at last there waz no abidin' in the place vor 'er':

30

He passed to the story of the laying . . . how seven parsons waited for Madam Carne in one of the passages, threw silk threads around her, and led her off to the pond. He explained: 'They waz bound to lay 'er under water, do ee zee; nort else wud keep 'er down; they'd tried buryin' 'er avore, an' that diddn do'.

The old man confessed to feeling a creepy sensation, like cold water running down his back, when he had been working in the field near the pond, and he said he knew plenty of people who didn't fancy working in that quarter. He told of a man who had a terrifying experience one night. In the dark he wandered off the footpath and came to the edge of the pond. All at once there was a swishing noise, and the water seemed blue with light. The narrator continued: 'This veller couldn't move vor vright. There waz a tremenjus noise, an' zummat riz up an' vlapped about an' then shot off up across the veeld'.

Next thing the man knew, he had fallen into the pond. He scrambled out and began running towards his home, but the 'tremenjus noise' came again, and he fell down in a faint. He lay on the ground all night in his wet clothes, and as a result was ill and off work for weeks.

Kille made his way to Withycombe church and stood before a memorial brass:

Here lyeth the bodie of Joane Carne, of Sandell, who was thrice married; first unto John Newton of Sandell, gent.; next unto Charles Wyndham Esquire; and last of all unto Thomas Carne of Eweny, in the county of Glamorgan, Esquire. She died on the nine and twentieth day of October 1612.

7 Somewhere between Heaven and Hell

'Not good enough for Heaven, not bad enough for Hell'. It sounds like a midway situation for millions of the human race, but Sir Arthur Quiller Couch had pixies in mind when he used the phrase in a poem.

Pixies, the little 'between' folk, are inseparable from Exmoor legend; they have left their name on copse and combe, meadow and mound, lane and glen, and their mark in the minds of Exmoor dwellers who used to lay claim to having been pixie-led.

Pixie legend was not for laughs, for that would have given offence to old Exmoor characters when they told their pixie tales. The 20th century indulges in a sceptical smile over the idea of pixies having an existence, but there was once a very real and widespread belief in the little folk. Many stories have filtered down the years. We hear of pixie-led people; of favoured farmers having their corn mysteriously threshed for them at night; of Withypool and Hawkridge as the domain of the monarch of the pixies; of the little folk sitting on Comer's Gate at Winsford Hill.

And even, told with a chuckle by the Central Electricity Generating Board in the nuclear age, how the pixies delayed the completion of the £70 million atomic power station at Hinkley Point, Stogursey!

Those capricious pixies! They would lure a body out of his way so that, unless he remembered to turn his coat or his pockets inside out, he could well wander all night, tumble into streams, stumble over humps, and fall into nettlebeds ere he found his homeward path again.

And what of the place-names for evidence? . . . Pixie Copse, near Bury; Pixie Meadow on East Lynch Farm, Selworthy; Pixie Lane at Minehead (now covered by The Parks Estate); Pixie Rocks in a Challacombe Glen; Pixie Piece and Pixies Mound, away from Exmoor at Stogursey.

The third Earl of Carnarvon said that the family seat at Pixton, Dulverton, was supposed to have been written at one time as 'Pixie Town'.

From The Angels?

How did pixie legends originate? One idea was that the little folk sprang from those angels who, in the general revolt led by Lucifer, were neither good enough for Heaven, nor bad enough for Hell. This is the idea used by Quiller Couch:

We were not good enough for Heaven,
Not bad enough for Hell,
And therefore unto us 'twas given
Unseen on earth to dwell

Unseen? Not always, according to some of the Exmoor tales! Perhaps there is a mixture of the possible and the impossible, of fact and fancy in the stories. Professor John Rhys, in his works on Celtic folklore, considers that some of the elements come from the worship of the imagination. Our Celtic ancestors, he suggests, projected on an imaginary world a primitive civilisation through which tradition represented their own race as having passed; or, more probably, a civilisation which they saw, or thought they saw, another race living. These, it is thought, were the people who had been conquered but not destroyed by the Celtic invaders, and who continued for long afterwards to live in scattered communities in the wilder parts of the country, as, for instance, on Exmoor. They were people of small stature and quick movement, who dwelt in low, turf-covered huts, and were able, by their traditional knowledge of secret ways through marsh and forest, to flit unnoticed from one place to another, stealing the cattle of their conquerors, kidnapping their children, carrying off their womenfolk. In time these earlier people died out or became absorbed in the dominant Celts or Saxons, but the traditions or superstitions that had grown up around them continued, indeed, outlived them by many generations.

In the face of the foregoing, one almost resents reading in F.J. Snell's *Book of Exmoor* how someone suggested to him that smugglers moving over Exmoor with contraband originated or deliberately fostered the pixie stories for their own ends, as a scare.

Pixie Land

Exmoor is true pixie land. Marwood de Winchelhalse, in *Lorna Doone*, says: 'No dog, no man, is the rule about here when it comes to coppice work; there is not a man who dare work here without a dog to scare the pixies'.

Dr. George F. Sydenham, of Dulverton, whose long practice on Exmoor made him conversant with people's beliefs in charms, superstitions and legends, referred to pixies when he addressed the West Somerset branch of the British Medical Association in 1900. He said: 'A belief in pixies is common; these little gentlemen have all sorts of pranks foisted on them; they ride our horses at night; they lure the man late home from market to take the wrong road on the moor, and compel him to dance all night with them in their fairy rings, to the sore distress of his affectionate wife, wearily waiting at home'.

Away From The Ding-Dongs

Exmoor pixie legends are a sheer delight. The king of the pixies ruled at Knighton Farm, in Withypool parish. Pixies have no love for consecrated places, and they detest the sound of church bells. One day the pixie king went to the Knighton farmer and asked for the loan of his packhorses and their crooks. 'I want to take my wife and family away from the noise of the ding-dongs', said the king.

And it was to Withypool farms that pixies came to thresh the corn at night. At one farm, curious womenfolk peeped through a hole in the barn door and saw the pixies busy threshing . . . in their birthday suits. So, to show gratitude for the services of the little folk, the women made clothes for them and left the gifts in the barn. The pixies took this as an insult, and they never came again.

Nuclear Age Disturbance

The pixies were reputed to have several haunts around Stogursey, notably in the Wick area, which was part of the 164 acres the Central Electricity Generating Board acquired for siting the first of two nuclear power stations. Several hitches occurred when No. 1 station was being built, and these were humorously ascribed, in the C.E.G.B. souvenir brochure issued for the station's opening ceremony, to the Wick pixies resenting man's disturbance of their traditional territory!

Pretty as a picture on the nursery wallpaper is another story from the same area. A ploughman heard the sound of crying and found a little 'peel' or baker's bread shovel, lying broken on the ground. He took it home, mended it, and returned it to the spot where he had found it. When he went there next morning it was gone, and in its place was a tasty little cake, straight from the oven of the little folk.

In a meadow in the Porlock Vale, so it is said, the pixies lighted little fires and dressed their children by them. But woe betide any human who was caught watching them. One luckless woman who was seen, said later that the pixies were so angry that they led her about all night over the moor and through the woods, and she did not reach home until daybreak. Porlock pixies seemed to like domestic service. They would enter a house at night through the keyhole, and in the morning the housewife would find everything beautifully clean. But the little folk expected a basin of bread and milk to be set out for them.

Blinded In One Eye

A woman at Minehead was said to have a male relative who had dealings with the pixies. One day she saw this relative in the market at Minehead, filching pieces of meat from the stalls. Going up to him, she said: 'Ah! I saw you'. 'Which eye did you see me with?' he asked. When the woman pointed to her right eye he blew upon it, and she never saw from it again!

34

Family Yarns

Three generations of an Exmoor family, the Needs, have been sources for pixie yarns. First, James Needs, of Mousehanger, near Bridgetown, who claimed to have been pixie-led. He was coming home from Dulverton, he said, and on arriving at the last field he must cross to reach his cottage he could not seem to find his way. He was led about by a pixie who carried a lantern. Jim made several attempts to knock the lantern with his stick, and succeeded at last in putting out the light and breaking the spell.

Jim's son, Jack, also of Mousehanger, could fascinate listeners with pixie yarns; he would tell of corn-threshing in the barns and the help the pixies gave, and how the women put out jugs of tea and plates of food for them. Jack had another story. A farmer who unwisely interfered with the pixies while they were at work was taught a severe lesson; they knocked him about with their flails.

At First-Hand

Thirdly, there was Jack's son, Charlie. He was the only man from whom Herbert Kille, of the *West Somerset Free Press*, obtained a first-hand account of a pixie-led experience. Charlie, a young man at the time, was living at Wellshead, Exford, and was on his way to his father's cottage at Mousehanger to return an umbrella. After getting a lift as far as Mounsey Hill Gate, he had to walk across South Hill to Broford Corner. The following is the adventure told in Charlie's own words:

There was a terrible wind blowing. I hadn't gone very far before my hat seemed to leave my head. I felt for it, and I found it was still there, but it seemed exactly as if it was off. I walked on, and suddenly I found myself in the middle of a great fuzz-bush. It was up to my chin. I could see a parting in the bush, but when I tried to get out there was none. I had heard folk tell about being pixie-led, and that if you turned your pockets inside out it would be all right. Well, I did that, and all at once I was out of the fuzz-bush. I found I was more than 400 yards off the path.

I found my way back to the path. It was only a sheep track, so I walked along the side of it. Then I thought I could hear something behind me, a pit-a-pat on the path. I stopped and listened, then went on, and I heard this sound again. I stopped three times, the third time, pit-a-pat, it came right up, and then I saw something beside me. I hit at it with the handle of my umbrella and saw it topple over. It was a little man with nothing on, like a baby out of its bath, and about two feet high. I was never so frightened in my life before. I took to my heels, and from there to the bottom of the hill there was no faster runner in England.

Traditionally a pixie haunt, was a wild combe between Challacombe and Chapman's Barrows. It earned the name Pixie Rocks, and people said the pixies dwelt among the crags jutting from the walls of the glen.

Jack O'Lantern

You could strike a match and explode a legend. The marsh gas would burn, destroying Jack o'Lantern before he could dance, exploding the legend in which our Exmoor forefathers believed . . . Jack as a will-o-the-wisp, whose leadings, like those of the pixies, could mean trouble for the led.

Jack o'Lantern was a little Exmoor fellow who lived deep in the boggy moorland and was more ubiquitous than the pixie, but his race has been practically extinguished by land drainage.

There never was very much to Jack, but being a wisp of a chap made him all the more legendary. Outside the airy-fairy realms he was merely a puff of marsh gas, but no-one would dream of reducing him to scientific terms in the hearing of Exmoor old-timers. He was part of their beliefs.

An old story has it that a Porlock farmer, making for Cutcombe via Dunkery, became benighted. Seeing a Jack o'Lantern, he appealed to it for help. 'Man a-lorst, man a-lorst', cried the farmer. 'Half a crown and a leg of mutton to show un the way to Cutcombe'.

Jack o'Lantern in story had two forms. One was as a pale-bluish light seen in churchyards and known as a corpse candle. A celebrated necromancer of the 16th century, Dr. Dee, of Manchester, is said to have been able to conjure a blue flame upon the brow of a corpse. But Jack o'Lantern in his other form and his marshy habitat, is a more understandable phenomenon. One hundred per cent land drainage would banish him for ever, and it is true that Jack o'Lantern sightings are rarely reported in present times. However, a century ago, as was recorded by F. T. Elworthy, a noted delver into lore and legend, Jack was a familiar night-light on the Brendons and Exmoor, playing his part in sustaining people's belief that their footsteps were sometimes strangely led.

Experiment

Not, for such people, the simple explanations, or the experiment that could be made with a box of matches. Near Brakely Steps, between Minehead and Porlock, was a pond where Jack o'Lantern could be tested . . . and become the laughing legend of natural gas. Prodding the bottom of the pond with a stick caused bubbles to rise to the surface, and if a lighted match was held close to them when they burst, they would catch fire. A puff or exhalation of gas behaving puckishly in the wind . . . and there we have Jack o'Lantern, or the *ignis fatuus*.

Jack's blue light fed the superstitions of Exmoor folk, especially on a breezy night. They voiced legends about his leadings. They would not have listened to an explanation that Jack's existence was caused by the slow burning of gas that had emanated from vegetable or animal matter decomposing in marshy water, or that the gas as it burned shared in the general movement of the air, so that the light seemed to dance.

Recumbent Effigy of de Brito(?) at St. George's, Sampford Brett *(see page 45)*
(H. H. Hole)

Brass Memorial to Joan Carne at St. Nicholas', Withycombe

HERE LYETH Y BODIE OF IOANE CARNE O
SANDELL WHO WAS THRISE MARRIED FIRST
VNTO IOHN NEWTON OF SANDELL GENT
AFTERWARD VNTO CHARLES WINDHAM
ESQVIRE AND LAST OF ALL VNTO THOMAS
CARNE OF EWENEY IN Y COVNTIE OF GLENERGA
ESQVIRE SHEE DYED ON Y NYNE & TWNTITH
DAYE OF OCTOBER IN THE YEARE OF OVR
LORD 1612

Stoke Pero Church

The Caratacus Stone, Winsford Hill

(Charles Whybrow)

The Gatehouse, Cleeve Abbey

8 The Devil on Exmoor

The Devil's appearances in Exmoor legend concern chiefly his great feats of sinew, his sportive moments when he has engaged in trials of strength with mythical giants, and his sundry influences on topography, such as creating Dunkery with one spadeful of earth . . . to leave a depression a few miles away at Winsford, known as the Punchbowl.

As a rock thrower, the Devil is beyond question the greatest of all. The writer, when a boy, was shown a huge, oblong, slab of stone in a valley, and received an old man's solemn assurance that the Devil flung it there from the distant Quantocks . . . in proof of which the man pointed to indentations at one end of the stone as the Devil's fingerprints!

Legend grants the busy Devil time off for such Olympic performances, and also ascribes to him numerous acts of vandalism to Nature's face when he has nothing better to do. For instance, he has operated spectacularly out in the Channel, being responsible for the Devil's Limekiln, that huge, triangular fissure of rock at the south end of Lundy Island. He did it by blowing the rock out of the earth and upending it in the sea nearby. His intention, of course, was that it should be forever a danger to the mariner. Thus was formed the Shutter Rock, which would just about fit into the Devil's Limekiln.

Author Charles Kingsley wrecked a Spanish galleon on the Shutter in his *Westward Ho!* but fiction turned cruel fact in 1910 when the British battleship, HMS *Montagu* (14,000 tons) grounded on the Shutter and became a total loss costing the taxpayers £2 million. There were no casualties among the 800 crew, most of whom were West Country men; one, Sydney Stenner, came from Exmoor.

Beware Tarr Steps

On a visit to Tarr Steps, the famous clapper causeway over the River Barle, it is well, should the day be warm and sunny, to take a quick peek before crossing to the other side. Make sure the Devil is not squatting on the stones. He holds the sunbathing rights at Tarr Steps. Unquestionably, since it was he who built the crossing.

An old woman who lived close by would never go over the steps until she had assured herself that the Devil was not a squatter. She came to know his likely times. On a sunless day a siesta was pointless; on the other hand, the Devil liked it not if the sun was too fierce. Understandably, he hankered for temperate conditions as a relief from the heat of the nether regions.

So the old woman would look out at the bridge from her cottage window and say: 'Ah! Th'ol Divil iddn there; thiccy stoan be too hot vur'n today. 'T'wud scald the backside feathers off un'.

Who would challenge the Devil's proprietary rights in Tarr Steps? After all, he carried every stone there in his huge apron, the strings of which finally gave way under the weight of a 20-tonner, and this one crashed by the side of the Barle.

His work done, the Devil hung up his apron in Hatt Wood and took to those sunbathing siestas, the while he mused upon his handiwork. He decided to keep the steps to himself, and vowed destruction upon any creature that should attempt to cross.

But Exmoor folk are enterprising. The locals sent a cat across. It was a complete sacrifice. The cat promptly disintegrated in a puff of smoke. Then a parson was prevailed upon to venture, and in the middle of the causeway he and the Devil came face to face. The confrontation began with the Devil using blue language that wilted the trees in Hatt Wood, but the parson, having done a great deal of private study, responded with an equally unprintable flow. This so impressed the Devil that he conceded Tarr Steps to the public for all time, excepting, of course, those suitable days when he would wish to sunbathe on the stones.

Punchbowl Appendix

Legend gives an appendix to the account of the Devil's exertions in creating Tarr Steps. Having finished, he climbed up to Winsford Hill and sat down to rest. He had become very thirsty and, as there was no stream handy, and he did not feel like returning to the Barle, he decided to dig for water.

Today, this would be called sinking a borehole; a permit would be required, and official notice of intention advertised in the Press. But the Devil was never thus circumscribed. Taking a spade, he cleared in one mighty heave an area now known as the Punchbowl, and there at the bottom was a stream of water.

What happened to the displaced soil? A very good question. The Devil flung the spadeful over his shoulder; it landed several miles off, and is seen today as Dunkery Hill!

It is the most natural thing to go laughing along with legend and call the Winsford depression the Devil's Punchbowl, but the Ordnance Survey does not use 'Devil' for prefix, as with Devil's Punchbowl near Hindhead in Surrey. In deference to legend, perhaps the addition should be made for Exmoor.

Battleship Basin

But while, in legend, the Devil created the Punchbowl, it was not called by that name until the early 19th century. According to F. J. Snell, in his *Book of Exmoor*, a Colonel Thornton, who lived at Dulverton and kept harriers, ran a hare across Bradley Bog and into the dip. Thornton was accompanied by his friend, Admiral Moresby, and they sat on the edge of the hollow, watching the hounds run the hare below. Thornton exclaimed: 'I say, Moresby, supposing that the hollow were baulked up at the other end like this, and filled with water, how many men-o'-war could ride comfortably there?' 'I should think', answered the admiral, 'three first-class ships of war might manoeuvre'. 'Then, egad!' rejoined his companion, 'Colonel Thornton has drunk as much port as could float three of His Majesty's seventy-fours'. When that story got around, the Punchbowl name for the dip was a certainty.

Blacksmith's Boast

Legend invests the Devil with a long stride that enables him to place one foot upon the Quantocks and the other on Exmoor. So it seems somewhat superfluous to equip him with a horse. But legend does. A coal-black charger, naturally.

At Keenthorne, a spot below the Quantocks, stands a dwelling that was formerly an extremely old forge. Here, a blacksmith claimed to have shod every horse for miles around and boasted that he would not mind having a go at the Devil's. Late one night the Devil rode up to the forge on his coal-black. The smith was abed, but the Devil hammered on the door, got him up, and demanded that he shoe the horse. The terrified smith, now regretting his boast, complied, but he refused to take the Devil's shilling in payment. Wise man. Thereby he saved his immortal soul.

Anger With The Church

It goes without saying that the Devil is not partial to churches. If, feeling in expansive mood, he allowed them to be built at all, he liked to decide the site himself, and would move stones from the chosen place, always, of course, by night. Such stories are told about several Exmoor churches, and it is well known in legend that St. Decuman's at Watchet, on a hill overlooking the town, is nowhere near the spot on which it was intended to erect it!

Such legends go deep into antiquity, so it is surprising to find one emanating from no more distant time than 1827. It concerns Wiveliscombe, where in that year the parishioners decided to demolish the ancient parish church and built the one that can be seen today. The original had got into a bad state of repair.

The Devil, who had happily watched its growing dereliction, was furious at the idea of a replacement that would mean a continuing expression of the Christian faith. Three days after the contract for the new church had been signed, a sad note was heard from the bells of the old. And strange sounds from within the church, as of spirits wailing over the doom of the habitation in which they had been lodged for so many centuries. When the door was opened a chill blast was felt, and a mist seemed to settle upon the sexton and the masons, who were much discomfited.

Personal Appearance

The wailings, chilly blast and mist, were but the prelude to the main performance. The Devil appeared in person, riding on a green dragon, in full view of the inhabitants. His wrath was terrible to behold. He reined his steed at a place called Coxborough, and taking up two great rocks, hurled them at the church tower. They rebounded and fell into a meadow, where they remained embedded.

It is probable that the Devil would have completed the demolition of the old church itself, there and then, had not the patron saint, Andrew, appeared with his cross. The Devil beat a retreat before the all-conquering sign.

Old Nick's personal appearances upon the stage of legend are no more. He moves insidiously among the great chorus of humanity, unseen, very much at work still, we may think. But that is never going to provide new legends to match the old fillibusters. Of course, if the Devil reverts to his old propensity for mighty labouring deeds, then we might see Dunkery put back into the Punchbowl!

9 A Coastal Path of Legend

Legend links two places to the west and east of Exmoor... Woolacombe sands and Flat Holm island. Between the two, William de Tracey must travel to do his penance.

His spirit was most likely on its way when the Flat Holm foghorn, the loudest in the Channel, began its blare. To an ear not attuned to legend it was merely a warning for fog-blinded mariners, but legend said its monotonous megaphone was the despairing moan of William de Tracey, leaving the island, his grave, once more to go to Woolacombe, there to begin a penance impossible of performance.

He must make bundles of sand and tie them with wisps of the same material! It was a penance to which he was condemned for his share in the murder of Archbishop Thomas à Becket. Other stints fell to his fellow knights in crime, de Brito, Morville and Fitzurse, but legend has particularised upon Tracey and his sand-binding. De Brito (or Brett) and Fitzurse were, like Tracey, West Country knights. Tracey belonged to Devon; de Brito and Fitzurse to places close by Exmoor. The cruciform church at Sampford Brett, where de Brito had his manor, is believed to have been founded as an act of penance for that dark deed in Canterbury Cathedral in 1170, and the chapel of ease at Williton, a half-mile from Sampford Brett, and now the parish church, was a similar founding by which it was hoped that the soul of Fitzurse could be purged.

A third church, Thorverton, in Devon, just off the Exe Valley road, is said to have been established as an act of reparation in the name of Tracey, but apparently it did not absolve him from that maddening task on Woolacombe sands. In 1970, the 800th anniversary of Thomas à Becket's murder was marked at Thorverton with a parade of 'Canterbury Pilgrims'.

Island Graves

Legend has given to two of the four knights, whose crime caused them to be execrated by all men, graves on Flat Holm. There is not a shred of evidence in support, but it would be a sorry day for legend, and would make this book superfluous, if evidence there was!

Flat Holm, sprawling in the grey waters of the Channel's shipping lane, has been considered a fit place for the graves of men whose hands bore the stain of unpardonable crime. Legend has put three of the knights there . . . Tracey, Fitzurse and de Brito . . . but fact shows only two graves!

Their existence had been known for centuries, but in a poem written in 1828 the Rev. William Lisle Bowles makes them three:

And there three mailed murderers retir'd
To the last point of land. Here they retir'd
And here they knelt upon the ground and cried
'Bury us 'mid the waves, where none may know
The whispered secret of a deed of blood'.

Bowles subsequently discovered that there were only two graves on the Holm, and he suggested they might be those of Fitzurse and Tracey.

Another curious feature is that the graves were dug north and south instead of the Christian way, east and west . . . an inference that those whose feet did not lie towards the morn would not be rising at the Resurrection. Bowles suggested that the burials may have been contrary to the usual direction of Christian graves, to express the point that murderers who smote the anointed Primate of the Holy Church should be consigned to oblivion.

Sanctuary?

Legend has allowed the spirit of William de Tracey to rise and leave Flat Holm for that periodical sand-binding penance at Woolacombe. Another legend makes the graves those of other offenders against the law, for there was a general belief that Flat Holm was for centuries a sanctuary for debtors and criminals seeking to escape the consequences of their misdeeds. There was an ancient custom of burying wrongdoers 'the wrong way about'.

Tracey must be left to his desperate dabbling on Woolacombe sands while we move eastward along the Exmoor coast to listen to legend's tongue in other places.

Glenthorne

Joseph of Arimathea and the young Christ setting foot on the Exmoor coast? A tendril of legend trails among the trees where the moor falls wildly beautiful to the Channel at Glenthorne, by County Gate. Curiously, it is a young tendril that seems to come from the very ancient parent tree of legend planted at Glastonbury, many miles away . . . the legend of Joseph of Arimathea sailing up the Channel to Glastonbury, planting his miraculous, thorn-blossoming staff on the Tor, and founding Christianity in England. A legend that is among the most cherished in Christendom. It says that Joseph came to Glastonbury years after the death of Christ, and that he reached the place after being warned in a dream not to stay his course along the Channel until he saw rising before him a hill 'most like to Tabor's mount'.

Obviously, that would rule out Glenthorne, far to the west, as a stopping place. But what if Joseph had sailed this way before, as a much younger man, bringing with him the young Christ? This, indeed, is what the Exmoor legend is about. It may have sprung—not a great many years ago—from the celebrated Glastonbury tale,

46

which has been in written record for some seven centuries. But Glenthorne's story is the word of mouth kind; it cannot be found in any record of lore or legend, and is probably unknown beyond the immediate area. It runs that Joseph and Christ came up the Channel in a trading ship which rough weather drove on to the beach at Glenthorne. Joseph and his charge walked up the combe searching for fresh water, and when they failed to find it Christ caused a spring to rise.

A never-failing spring, declared a woman who lived at County Gate. Daily she fetched water from it.

Sir William's Surprise

The late Sir William Halliday, of Glenthorne House, to whom the author referred the legend in 1964, replied that he had not known of it, although the spring was on his property. He was disposed to regard the story as a comparatively modern 'manufacture' for the benefit of tourists greedy for local lore, and said that at least it was a change from 'the usual Lorna Doonery'!

Sir William added: 'There is a stream which rises below County Gate on the north side, provides the cottages with water, and runs down to the sea through my garden, forming the county boundary. It is joined on the way by another stream from a spring rising two-thirds of the way up Glenthorne Combe. This spring is covered by a stone dome with a cross on top, and the water emerges through a marble trough which came from one of the Greek islands. The affair was constructed by the builder of Glenthorne, the Rev. Walter Stephen Halliday, who delighted in such ornaments and curios, and he called it The Sisters' Fountain in honour of his three sisters'.

From a dome topped by a cross, it may have been but a short step in someone's thinking to start the story of a Christian miracle.

Porlock

Moving along the coast to Porlock, we encounter the legend of Lucote, a bully who had to be cut down to size. It was done so successfully that at the end he could be squeezed into a little tin box, but he gave a whole heap of trouble before that stage was reached.

Lucote lived near Porlock church, was a braggart as well as a bully, and was so heartily disliked that his death spread relief throughout the village. Short-lived relief, for a week after his funeral he reappeared, as bullying and insulting as ever.

Obviously, he would have to be 'laid', but it must be apparent from previous chapters that exorcisms have a habit of going wrong. So it was in the case of Lucote. Eleven parsons gathered in the parish church with bell, book and candle. They exorcised the bully most fearfully, only to hear a loud laugh at the conclusion of the cere-monies. And there, leering from behind a pillar, was Lucote. He

47

advanced upon the parsons, and as they fled in terror he bellowed belligerently after them.

Eleven Plus One

There was apparently some mystique in numbers. The eleven discomfited parsons thought they might do better if they became twelve, so they prevailed on the parson of St. Decuman's, Watchet, to join them. Again they went through the exorcism, intensifying the cursing, yet the end was the same . . . Lucote's derisive bellow was heard, and he advanced up the nave in a most threatening attitude.

It was the St. Decuman's parson who stood his ground and saved the day . . . and the future. He gave Lucote a verbal flaying, and the bullying spirit subsided for the moment. But that was not enough. The parson knew he must press home the advantage. He began to taunt Lucote. 'You are a boasting bully', he said, 'and I am only half your size, but I can do more than you can. I'll warrant you cannot even chew this biscuit I have under my cloak'.

Lucote began to roar. 'If you cannot prove your words I will tear you limb from limb, and the other priests with you. But if you prove what you say, I will submit. It is a bargain'.

'Done', said the parson. 'And if you fail to chew the biscuit I give you, you will obey my orders and never plague Porlock again'.

Duped

The parson produced a little cake and told Lucote it was one of the biscuits Watchet people were noted for making. The parson bit it, swallowed a piece, and then put it to Lucote's lips. 'Your turn', he said.

Lucote bit, and there was a strange development. He began to tremble and groan, and spat out the pieces of biscuit. Ah! That crafty parson. Lucote knew he was finished. It was not a biscuit at all, but the holy wafer, the Host itself, used in the Mass at St. Decuman's the previous Sunday. Obviously, it would not agree with Lucote.

'Come with me', said the parson to Lucote, who was now as meek as a lamb. 'I have a horse for you outside the church. You will ride away with me'.

The pair rode through the night, past Minehead, Dunster and Blue Anchor, and beyond Watchet to the shore at Doniford. Dawn was breaking as they dismounted. The parson laid a little tin box upon a rock, opened it, and said to Lucote, 'This is for you. In you go'.

To Tom Thumb Size

Meekly, Lucote stood upon the box and immediately began to dwindle . . . smaller and smaller, and thinner, until he sank right into the box. Then the parson snapped the lid shut and put the sign of the Cross upon it.

He doomed Lucote to depart in the box on the next tide, as far as the Red Sea, there to remain for a thousand years. After that time he would be allowed to come back to Porlock, but his journey must be at the rate of a cockstride a year.

The tide came in and snatched the box, and that was that. Lucote is understood to be somewhere east of Suez, and Porlock is a very nice place in which to live.

Carhampton

In 1970, the parish of Carhampton, which has a seabord at Blue Anchor, engaged in a long argument over finding a name for a new housing estate. Ultimately, the local council fell back on legend and named the estate 'Carantoc', after the 6th century Celtic saint who is supposed to have landed there from Wales.

Here is legend with the kind of embroidery the old monks liked to work. St. Carantoc, while in Wales, had taken possession of an altar of wondrous colouring that had been cast down from Heaven. He was bringing it across the Channel when it fell from his boat and was lost, so he made his way to King Arthur at Avalon and asked if the altar had come ashore anywhere. Arthur said it had, but that Carantoc, before he could claim it, would have to perform a great deed.

This was no less than the capture of a fierce serpent that lived in a morass by the shore at Blue Anchor and was terrorising the neighbourhood. (The name of this place today is Ker, or Car, Moor.) Carantoc went to the edge of the morass and called the serpent, which obediently came out. 'Then', says a legend probably written by a monk's hand, 'Carantoc cast his stole about the serpent and brought it to the hall where King Arthur and his nobles sat, and fed it there. Then he let it go, bidding it to do no more harm to man or beast.'

Reclaimed

So Carantoc was able to reclaim his lost altar. Privately, King Arthur may have been a trifle reluctant to let it go, for he had purposed making it into a table for himself and his knights.

Carantoc built a church to hold his altar. Leland, King Henry VIII's antiquary, must have been familiar with the legend, for when he journeyed through Somerset he wrote of Carhampton as 'Carantoke's Town, where yet is a chapel of this saint'.

The legend takes a knock because the present church at Carhampton is dedicated to St. John The Baptist. However, when the foundations for the vicarage were being dug, traces were found of a building that may have been Carantoc's oratory.

Watchet

The coastal path of legend ends at Watchet. Borne in upon legend's tide, here comes St. Decuman, whose name is given to the parish church high above the town.

Like Carhampton's Carantoc, Watchet's Decuman was a Celtic saint who came across the Channel as a missionary of the Gospel. One of our heathen ancestors slew him, thereby adding gorily to legend, for the saint calmly picked up his severed head and washed away the blood in the waters of a spring near where the church was to be built. Then he put his head back on.

The spring, known as St. Decuman's holy well, has been fenced and protected through the interest of members of the Wyndham family. The resurrected lady Florence of an earlier chapter would have passed it that night on her way home to Kentsford from the church vault.

Legend gives the Decuman story a pretty detail. The saint crossed the Channel on a hurdle, accompanied by a cow which followed him about and supplied him with milk.

A 19th century sexton at Watchet had it gloriously jumbled when he answered a visitor's question, 'Who was St. Decuman?'

'A saint as lived at I donnoware in Wales, where um cut his head off, but un stuck on again, zur, not mab-be straight, tho', an' then made a boat of hes cloak, tho' zum du zay 'twaz a whurdle, an' com'd across the zea. An' hur had a cow that follerd un an' giv'd un milk. An hur lived in a cave an' bilded the church'.

50

10 A Shortened Form of Matins

Sometimes, legend is a growth around a slim fact. Happily, seldom a malignant growth. More often, fat with humour.

So, what *did* happen one Sunday morning at Stoke Pero, when at service time the church key could not be found?

Fact there was, but in the telling, legend may have taken control. The basis was that 'a sort of service', with a prayer or two but no sermon, was held in the farmhouse adjoining the church when the key to the door of this mountain house of prayer was mislaid. Nothing in that for merriment . . . until the verbal growth of legend and its ultimate appearance in print.

Holding the story in hand for a moment, we take a look at little Stoke Pero, sternly ridged on the northern side of Dunkery. It is probably one of Exmoor's most ancient Christian emplacements, yet it receives only the scantiest note in historical record. Writers have given it little respect; its right to exist at all seems to have raised inquiring eyebrows. A man living in get-at-able Porlock down below is said to have told a traveller who asked him the best way to get to Stoke Pero, 'There's no best way'.

Up The Mountains

Locke, engaged on his Somerset Survey, came to Stoke Pero in 1795 after 'scaling mountains which hath narrow paths encumbered with large loose stones'. He saw a place that did not seem worth the trouble it had put him to in getting there: that is, judging by his observation of a church plus 'fourteen mean-looking dwellings, rack-rented'. Locke may have thought, also, that he had reached a primitive outpost of murder and mayhem when the parish clerk told him that the ale-selling licence once held there by a woman had been taken from her 'because she had married every farmer in the parish and buried them all within ten yards of the cellar door'. An Exmoor humorist was merely putting a riddle to Locke. It meant that the only two farmers in the little parish had married the woman licensee, had died before her, and were buried in the church-yard adjoining the public house, which was later called Church Farm.

Exmoor's goodly provision for humans from its earth and stock combine to give Stoke Pero one of the best of many local bell legends.

'Milk, crame and 'orts
Say the bells of Stoke church'

And rhymster's licence drew, of old, three isolated parishes into a somewhat slanderous couplet:

'Culbone, Oare, Stoke Pero,
Parishes three where no parson'll go'

There may have been pastoral staffing problems at various times in the long history of these upland parishes, but in the mid-19th century Stoke had its own incumbent, the Rev. Robert Freke Gould, and he it was who figured, with a farmer named Heywood, in the incident of the mislaid church key. Thereby was born the tale that oft-telling was to make legendary.

Which Sunday?

After an unvailing search for the key, it was decided to make some attempt at holding matins in the adjoining farmhouse. There is no doubt that the service began . . . and no doubt that worship tailed off in an atmosphere that was not conducive to it. 'A service with a prayer or two but no sermon' has been a true description; it is the in-filling that contributes the legend. We are invited to believe that parson and clerk knew not which Sunday this was; that an argument arose between them as to which psalm was due for recital; and that it was settled by Farmer Heywood consulting Old Moore's almanack.

The service reached the responses stage, in which the clerk was supposed to intone 'O Lord, shew Thy mercy upon us'. Instead, and with a nice regard for the surroundings, he allegedly said 'O Lord, look down dru the thatch 'pon top o' us'. A classic little sample of a ready, native skill for improvisation.

The chance of these farmhouse matins reaching their appointed end was extremely remote. Legend gives us the tiny congregation eventually at ease in front of the fire, smoking, and drinking the farmer's cider.

The tale remained a verbal chuckle on Exmoor for some 25 years; then, in 1888, it was told in print. One 'Somerset Frank' (as he signed himself) set it forth as a humorous dialect piece in the *West Somerset Free Press*.

Repudiated

Dialect gilded 'Somerset Frank's' account of 'zum zart o' a zar-viss', the argument about the right 'zaam' to recite, and the final spectacle of the tiny congregation 'a-zot roun' the vire, smawkin' an' swiggin' zider'.

There were repercussions. Relatives of Parson Gould warmly repudiated the story as an absurdity, saying that it did not reflect at all charitably upon the clergyman, and pointing out that he was a non-smoker during his 27 years at Stoke Pero. And, added the writers, with a kind of knock-out punch, the farmer could not possibly have consulted the almanack, he being unable to read!

But the wings of legend, having left the facts grounded and lost at Stoke Pero 25 years before, were not now to be clipped!

11 Trying for Treasure

Buried treasure! Legendary or real, it matters not; the lure is there. Treasure is an exciting word that used to send schoolboys searching a library's fiction shelves. But the hunts do not all belong to fiction; nor do all relate to times long past.

The Caractacus Stone

Why was Exmoor's famous inscribed monument of the Dark Ages—the Caractacus Stone on Winsford Hill—mysteriously moved less than 40 years ago? An abortive attempt to dig for treasure that, legend says, is lying under the stone?

This affair, in 1936, alarmed archaeologists. For some 1,500 years, perhaps longer, the stone had stood close to two roads . . . relatively unharmed until, late in the 19th century, some fractures were caused by a cart's impact, and a piece of the stone hacked off with a pick in a labourer's idle moment. The 1936 incident, in which the seven hundredweight stone was prised from its foundations and left lying on the ground, received widespread notice, for by that time the Caractacus was no longer just an old stone known only to local farmers and to the sheep which rubbed themselves against it. It had been declared the most important landmark of its kind in Somerset. Indeed, an eminent Celtic scholar, Professor Sir John Rhys, had classed it as one of the most important monuments in South-West England. J. Ll. Warden Page, the Williton author and antiquary, had awakened public interest in the Caractacus in 1890, and in the years between the two World Wars Alfred Vowles, of Minehead, never happier than when he was nosing on Exmoor, had made the stone a special study and the object of his very practical interest.

Midnight Waggon

Ancient legend survived . . . that treasure lay under the stone. F. J. Snell, in his book, *The Blackmore Country*, writes of the Winsford Hill locale: 'Around these spots cluster superstitions weird and bizarre. The menhir (stone) is an index of buried treasure'.

Old folk recalled a story that around midnight a waggon and horses could be heard crossing the moor, taking away the treasure. Gipsies who used to camp on Winsford Hill had also been familiar with this tale, and they embellished it with an account of the waggon hitting the stone and turning over; another, of the carter being killed.

Yes, in story the dark folds of Winsford Hill by night bred tremors.

At Comer's Gate were pixies; at Wambarrows lurked the black dog apparition, so familiar in lore. Exmoor folk shunned the hill when evening had fallen.

Yet the Caractacus had visitors on an October night in 1936, and by coincidence, Alfred Vowles was one of the first to learn of the incident. He had told an acquaintance, who had never seen the Caractacus, but was going to a meet of the staghounds at Winsford Hill on October 17th, that this would be a good chance to look at the stone. This man met Vowles on October 20th and told him he had been to the Caractacus site and found the stone lying on the ground.

Not Vandalism?

Vowles was astounded. After reporting the matter to H.M. Office of Works and the National Trust, he went to the site. The great stone had been prised up with the use of heavy implements, judging by the marks in the disturbed soil. There had been no attempt to deface the stone or its inscription, which seemed to rule out vandalistic intention, leaving the inference that the culprits must have been seeking the legendary treasure. It was suspected that the manpower and tools necessary for such heavy work had been available within the locality, and intensive police inquiries were made. They came to nothing.

The stone was carted to a safe place until the Office of Works could arrange for its re-setting, and meanwhile a watch was kept on the site to prevent digging by treasure seekers or souvenir hunters. The stone was replaced in June the following year. The work was arranged by H. St. George Gray, who directed many archaeological excavations in Somerset. James Steer, a Winsford contractor, supplied the labour.

Opportunity to search the sub-soil for any objects of archaeological interest was taken before the stone was re-set. The result was a message for the treasure hunters of that October night, or others with similar ideas . . . 'Don't waste your time. There's nothing under the Caractacus'!

Monksilver

The south aisle of Monksilver parish church was built in the 16th century from funds provided by a blacksmith who had chanced upon a sackful of gold.

So runs a treasure legend upon which generations of Monksilver villagers were reared. And they would point to some stained glass in the south aisle window, where 'blacksmith's tools' are depicted . . . hammer, nail, pair of pincers, horseshoe.

It is said that a local blacksmith sent to Bristol for an hundredweight of iron, and in due time received a sack filled with metal. Opening it, he was astonished to find it full of glistening gold. In gratitude for this sudden wealth, he put up the funds to add a south aisle to his parish church, and his trade device was incorporated in a window design. An old writer has commented facetiously that Bristol was a city so rolling in riches, that the man who inadvertently consigned a sack of gold instead of a sack of iron to a humble blacksmith in West Somerset, either never missed it or could not be bothered to rectify the error!

Debunking

Alas for this legend. It has suffered a double debunking this century. Ecclesiastics have pointed out that the devices which supposedly commemorate the lucky blacksmith more likely represent emblems of the Passion, often found in churches. The legend became further frayed when someone drew attention to the fact that the hammer device in the Monksilver window is a claw type, and that claw-hammers were unknown before the 19th century. It appeared, therefore, that this stained-glass must date from about 1845, when the church underwent a restoration. Another nail was driven into legend's coffin in 1948, when the Dean of York and the Bishop of Zanzibar visited Monksilver, thinking they were going to see the blacksmith's tools in 15th or 16th century stained-glass. They were surprised to find they were looking at the stained-glass work of John Toms, a mid-19th century expert, of Wellington!

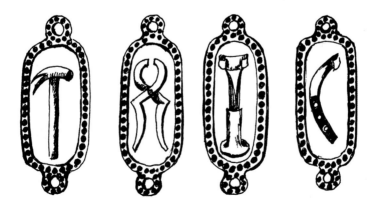

Broomfield

A spur of the Quantock Hills provides a buried treasure legend . . . a vast store of wealth lying in an underground castle. The parish is Broomfield, where, in a candle-power age, Andrew Crosse's experiments in electricity brought down upon him the wrath of the villagers, who were convinced that either he was leagued with the Devil, or was a sorcerer in his own right.

But much older than this period is the legend of the parish money field. The wealth is within a castle of iron, guarded by spirits. It is true that at one time an underground passage existed, but it was closed up a great many years ago, and the field planted over. Legend said that the door to the castle could be located only at full moon. A story that some labouring men, in curiosity and hope, once engaged in a dig in the money field, is probably true. Less credible is the embellishment . . . that they desisted from their task on account of the mournful sounds that came up to them from wailing spirits!

Doctor's Try

From this point, legend really takes over. A local doctor, greatly learned in books, discovered by study how to get into the underground castle. On the day before the full moon he went over the field, using a hazel rod as a diviner. When he was directly over the castle door, the rod stood upright in the ground.

Late that night he returned with his servant and tools for digging, and eventually the spade struck on the iron door of the castle. At once, horrible groans and cries were heard, and spirits began to emerge from the door. One caught the servant by the leg and would have carried him off, but the doctor put a Bible on the man's head and dragged him out and away with the other hand. The pit closed up, the door banged shut, and its position was changed so that it would never be found again.

Cleeve Abbey

Around the ancient stones of the Cistercian abbey of Cleeve, at Washford, has circled a legend of buried treasure ever since the last abbot quit the abbey at the time of the Dissolution. With it goes a story of a dig for trove at the beginning of the 19th century.

Legend says that, before Cleeve's abbot went away in 1539, he buried plate and other monastic treasures under the shadow of the abbey church tower. The church was part of the conventual buildings, and as all Cistercian churches had a central tower, it was presumed that the treasure must lie in the north or south transept.

Around 1800, a tenant farmer of the abbey lands concluded that a bit of digging in the abbey ruins might be more profitable than a whole lot of farming. So he put a gang of labourers on the job. After a long dig they came down upon a barrel. This was the moment for the farmer to show his cunning. He told the men to suspend labours and go with him to the farmhouse for a cider session. His intention, it is said, was to ply them with his most potent libation until they were drunk; he would then go out to the church on his own, knock in the head of the buried barrel, and find out what was inside before anyone else knew a thing about it.

Intervention

However, there was a startling intervention. While the men were at the cider jar they were frightened by a loud crash. The old tower had fallen in, filling the hole they had excavated, and effectually burying the treasure cask. They refused to have anything more to do with the job. They could have shifted the fallen stones, but they regarded the tower's fall as a token of the Almighty's displeasure with them for their part in an act of sacrilege. No attempt was ever again made to unearth the treasure.

Respect for sacred precincts was more apparent in olden times than it is today. But Cleeve Abbey had not seen its last dig, and although one conducted in the present century was not for treasure, it illustrated men's reluctance to meddle in holy spheres, and their deep-rooted belief in spirits.

Just before the 1914-18 war, Sir William St. John Hope arrived at Cleeve for archaeological research, and he engaged a party of local labourers as diggers. From the start, there were murmurs. The men said it was a Friday, and therefore unlucky to be starting the job; that the place was known to be riddled with spirits, and that while it was one thing to dig a drain, it was quite another to disturb dead men's bones.

Situation Handled

Sir William handled the awkward situation in masterly style. He assured the men that no bones would be disturbed, and that Friday, far from being a dangerous day, was particularly immune from the visitations of spirits . . . especially when a man was digging really hard!

That did it. Frightened men turned into a party of Trojans. Digging furiously for six days, unhampered by spirits, they laid bare Cistercian history and added to archaeological record the details of a quite remarkable 12th century drainage system!

57

12 Did Tom Faggus Really Ride?

Between fact and legend lies a fascinating, often frustrating strip of ground for contention. Upon it, two people may argue Doones to the point of exhaustion. But with no conclusiveness. The same goes for Tom Faggus, the Claude Duval of Exmoor. Did he really ride the moorland roads, a gallant plunderer, on his comely Winnie, the strawberry roan mare? Or are horse and man merely dimensionless drawings in the print of a novel?

Tom Faggus is a minor figure in Blackmore's *Lorna Doone;* in character and exploit built up in the stories Exmoor people of the 18th and 19th centuries told about him, he exists in his own right. He can be independent of *Lorna Doone.* And perhaps there is more reality to him than to the Doones or lovely Lorna.

It can hardly be doubted that he, or someone like him, had a real existence as a romantic highwayman, yet when the matter comes to the test, the incontrovertible proof is missing. No research into the Faggus story has produced that last bit of evidence in black and white which alone will satisfy the conscientious historian . . . an entry in a church register, either of Tom's birth or his marriage, or his name in any document pertaining to land or property. And if, as the stories say, Tom was hanged, there should be a record of that end and of his trial. There is none. In *Lorna Doone* Tom does not hang; he gets a pardon and a new deal in society.

Top Value

If Faggus was real, then the exploits with which he is credited make him legendary as well! If he did not exist, he is still top value as legend. As Blackmore says in his novel: 'Since Tom Faggus died, there has not been such a man to be found, nowhere round these parts'.

But in addition to what we may learn through *Lorna Doone,* there are other pointers to examine along the road to finding Faggus.

He registers in story as a North Molton native. As a young man he worked there as a blacksmith and was a first-class craftsman. The forge, pulled down about 50 years ago, stood opposite the old Poltimore Arms Inn. Tradition says that Tom, though but a smith, was no country boor. He could read and write, and he had what Blackmore calls 'solid substance' . . . a piece of land worth a hundred pounds, and right of common of 200 sheep and a score and a half of beasts.

Dire Misfortune

Tom loved a South Molton maid, Betsy Paramore, and they were about to get married. But dire misfortune struck. Tom became involved in a lawsuit with Sir Robert Bampfylde and lost everything he possessed. Embittered, he turned gentleman-robber, and for many years 'collected contributions on the highway, sometimes with a companion named Penn, but more frequently alone'. He operated in accord with the heroic model of those times, sparing the poor, relieving the sick, but plundering without mercy the rich of their cash and valuables. He was never guilty of bloodshed, and he never insulted a woman. There we have all the accepted qualifications of highwayman romance.

Tom became as adept in his new line as he had been skilful in his blacksmith's trade. Blackmore says he made a fine reputation! 'All good people liked him . . . when he had not robbed them, and many a poor sick man or woman blessed him for other people's money'!

He is said to have held up Sir Robert Bampfylde, the man who had ruined him. Having relieved the knight of his purse and jewellery, Tom handed them back, saying cuttingly that it was against all usage for him to rob a robber.

Sharp Wit

Of Tom's coolness, daring, and sharpness of wit, the stories are many. For instance, there is his encounter with a band of armed men who had gathered at Exford in the hope of capturing him. Tom rode up to them with a grave demeanour. Protruding from his coat pocket was a long piece of paper. The party took him for a gentleman. He declared that he held His Majesty's commission to capture a notorious rogue, by name Thomas Faggus. When the party said they were waiting for this very man, Tom asked them what firearms they had, and they produced their guns, whereupon Tom suggested that as the priming might be damp the guns ought to be discharged and reloaded, to ensure that they went off properly when they were really needed for firing. So the men fired their guns into the air, and Tom whipped out a pair of pistols and terrified the party by declaring his identity. He relieved them of all their money, cast it to the poor old folk standing round, and galloped off.

The Enchanted Mare

This is a suitable point for introducing Winnie, Tom's 'enchanted strawberry mare', so fleet of foot, so beautiful, so sagacious and faithful in helping her master whenever he was hard pressed.

It is a point, also, to introduce a letter that seems to indicate a real existence for Tom Faggus. Journalist Herbert Kille had frequently gone 'in search of Faggus' by means of various lines of inquiry. Very near he got . . . but, like everybody else, never quite there.

In 1943 Kille received a letter from Mr. Alexander Luttrell, of Dunster Castle and Court House, East Quantoxhead. Mr. Luttrell wrote: 'About 70 years ago a farmer from Exmoor came to Dunster Castle to tell my father (Mr. George Fownes Luttrell) of a mare he had for sale. My father asked questions; among them, what was the mare's colour? The farmer replied, 'Her be Faggus colour, your Honour'.

'And by this', Mr. Alexander Luttrell added, 'my father knew the mare to be a strawberry roan'.

Mr. Luttrell also drew Kille's attention to a narrow meadow, well hidden, in the woods at Combe Sydenham, Monksilver, which had long gone by the name 'Faggus Mead'. Here, according to tradition, Faggus kept a horse.

Leap From The Bridge

In that most famous of Faggus stories, his leap into the River Taw from Barnstaple Bridge to avoid capture, the courage and devotion of Winnie the mare are exemplified. On another occasion Tom was in an alehouse at Simonsbath when the place was surrounded, and he was like to be taken prisoner. At the sound of a shrill whistle from her master the mare broke down the stable door and scattered the crowd outside the house by a savage attack with her hooves. Tom leapt on her back and galloped away to safety. A similar incident has Porlock for its locale.

Tom's activities covered a wide area; stories have been gathered from the Barnstaple district on the one side of Exmoor and from Minehead on the other. It was at an Alcombe smithy that he was supposed to have persuaded the farrier to turn the shoes of the strawberry mare 'front ways avore', so that his pursuers would be misled.

The Fire-Fork

When Barnstaple Corporation established a museum at St. Anne's chapel in the parish churchyard, they put among the exhibits a fire-fork believed to have been the property of Tom Faggus. It was presented by Mr. Bruce Oliver, to whom it was given by Miss Yeo, of Yeoldon, Swimbridge. Her house at that time incorporated an old kitchen, traditionally that of Tom Faggus.

In 1929 Herbert Kille wrote to Bruce Oliver and received the following reply: 'Of proof there is none. But let us take the point of view that if it isn't Tom Faggus's fire-fork, it ought to be. The certainties are that it is an old fork; that it came out of a house traditionally claimed to be Tom Faggus's; as far as living memory goes it has always remained in the house'.

60

The fire-fork figures in the following story: Tom was seen returning home while most of the people of Swimbridge were at service in their parish church. Someone ran to the church door shouting 'Tom Faggus be coming 'ome', and the congregation left and hurried to the house, making a ring around it. Tom saw them coming, and as usual his wits served him well. Putting his hat on the fire-fork, he pushed it out of the chimney top. 'There he be', shouted a man. 'He be trying to get out of the chimbley'. A man with a gun fired at the hat, which dropped. 'Come on, Faggus be daid', was the cry, and everybody ran for the front door. Tom nipped out at the back, mounted his mare, and was gone.

Pardon . . . Or The Rope?

In *Lorna Doone* we have Faggus obtaining a pardon 'when a new king arose', and thereafter living 'a godly and righteous (though not always sober) life, and bringing up his children to honesty as the first of all qualifications'.

Therein, Blackmore departs from the traditional history of Faggus, which does not give a happy ending to his adventurous career. 'Black care rides behind the horseman', says the poet, and Faggus was no exception to the rule. He was at last taken by a stratagem in an ale-house at Exebridge. An officer disguised as a beggar entered the room in which Tom sat, and the highwayman, with his customary kindness, gave the supposed beggar alms and ordered food for him. The beggar tipped Tom over, slipped a rope around his feet, and hoisted him to the ceiling. In order to break through the 'enchantment' that surrounded the strawberry mare, other minions of the law shot her at the same moment her master was suspended, and the whistle he gave for her to come to his aid was in vain.

If, all along, the reader has been feeling a sneaking regard for Tom, this is the moment to feel a distaste for the law!

Tradition says that Tom was duly tried, condemned and hanged. Again, no record of this can be found.

The Name

In 1936, Herbert Kille, still pursuing Faggus, wrote to an old-established firm of solicitors in South Molton, but they told him they had never come across the name Faggus or any variations of it in that district. Around the same time, the Rev. W. J. Prew, Vicar of South Molton, informed Kille that he had been unable to discover a Faggus in the registers. The nearest name to Faggus is probably Fugars; it appears on a stone in the kitchen of Court Farm, Exford . . . 'Thomas Fugars. 1674. Anne'. Local tradition has associated this with Tom Faggus, but it is more likely to refer to Thomas Furgers or Fugars, of Minehead, who died there in 1677. The Fugars family can be traced back to 1539, and they seem to have been perfectly respectable.

In addition to Faggus Mead, previously mentioned, there is a spot in Chargot Wood, Luxborough, known as Faggus Stable. It was mentioned in an advertisement for a timber sale in 1892. Faggus Stable was one of several similar places where Tom might have kept his horse, or hidden himself and the horse to await the coming of a coach along the adjacent highway.

Long Way Back

The Tom Faggus yarns were probably in circulation more than 150 years before *Lorna Doone* was published in 1869. And there is evidence that they were in manuscript form about 1840. Who was the original storyteller? Very likely, Ursula Babb (1738-1826). Her grandfather, John Babb, figures in *Lorna Doone* as the man who captured Major Wade. Assuming the existence of the Doones, and that they were cleared from Exmoor in the last few years of the 17th century, it means that Ursula Babb was born only about 40 years after this 'good riddance' event. In terms of people's memory and the handing on of tales, 40 years must surely mean that the Doone and Faggus stories were still fresh and clear.

Tom Faggus, highwayman, is strong enough to lead an existence independent of the Doone romance. He rides in legend with perhaps more substance than a Doone. He would ride in actual fact . . . if only a line in a register or official document would come to light.

With a sense of frustration, we have to leave Tom astride his strawberry mare on a distant Exmoor horizon of legend. Close we may get, but never quite close enough to put out a hand and seize Winnie by the bridle of fact.

62

13 The Naked Boy takes a Walk

The midnight hour is for dark witching. Drained is the fairy godmother's power, so that the glittering princess flees the ballroom as the ragged Cinderella once more.

Strange powers take over as midnight chimes. Ornamental lions which, during daytime, have been immobile and immutable upon the gateways to ancestral homes, come to life and pad off to the nearest stream to take a drink.

And on the Brendon Hills the Naked Boy moves across the fields. Like the lions, he needs refreshment from the spring.

Here is ancient lore . . . that stone landmarks walk; equally ancient, the legend that specifies the Naked Boy as one of them.

The name is one of the most intriguing of the many that dot the Exmoor area map. The Naked Boy (except when missing at midnight!) stands 1,300 feet above sea level where four parishes meet . . . Treborough, Withiel Florey, Old Cleeve and Brompton Regis. It measures four feet above ground level, and has a ground level circumference of twelve feet.

Curious

In 1822 the stone, which must have been standing there for centuries, was curiously map-marked in the plural as 'Four Naked Boys', but it was as a walking-stone in the singular that people on the Brendon Hills put it into legend. The Naked Boy, they said, was an inveterate old drunkard who for his sins was turned into stone, and still, for his sins, he must go down to drink at a brook at midnight, even in his petrified state.

Similar legends attach to standing stones in other parts of the country. The Banbury stone goes down to the River Avon to drink when the church clock strikes twelve, and several menhirs in Brittany go one better . . . they perform ablutions in the river! The curious obsession for drink and washing is unexplained, and the legends probably have their origin in a folk memory of moving stones going back to times when primitive man believed that stones were living things. A boundary stone at Putts Corner, dividing the parishes of Sidbury and Gittisham in Devon, chooses midnight on Christmas Eve to go down to the sea, and a stone slab of Celtic origin at Margam takes itself off to the sea on Christmas morning! Always, the pattern of legend is the same . . . the stone going to find water, fresh or salt.

Beating The Bounds

Although the Naked Boy of the Brendons marks the meeting point of parishes, it was probably there long before parish boundaries were defined, serving as a mark stone to guide travellers along the primitive tracks. Its name must have come from the ritual of beating the bounds in centuries past. It is well authenticated that on such occasions (for instance, the perambulation of Exmoor Forest) a primitive custom of impressing the event and the limits of parishes on the minds of the bounds-beaters prevailed. It took the form of a sharp physical reminder. Very likely, the Naked Boy stone attracted its name because one of the youngsters present was stripped of his clothes and made to stand on the stone or walk around it. At 1,300 feet up, this could be a chilling as well as embarrassing experience for a lad, one he would be unlikely to forget.

The four parishes which touch at Naked Boy may each have supplied a 'victim' for the bounds-beating; there seems no other explanation for the 1822 map-markers naming the stone 'Four Naked Boys'.

One man might well have moralised upon the legend of the Naked Boy as a petrified drunkard doomed to a midnight walk to slake his thirst in water. He was the Rev. Dr. Henry Gale, Rector of Treborough, one of the 19th century's most vocal campaigners against the liquor trade.

The Naked Boy was his parishioner!